T0222858

A Complete Guide to Burp Suite

Learn to Detect Application Vulnerabilities

Sagar Rahalkar

Apress®

A Complete Guide to Burp Suite

Sagar Rahalkar
Pune, Maharashtra, India

ISBN-13 (pbk): 978-1-4842-6401-0
https://doi.org/10.1007/978-1-4842-6402-7

ISBN-13 (electronic): 978-1-4842-6402-7

Managing Director, Apress Media LLC: Welmoed Spahr
Acquisitions Editor: Divya Modi
Development Editor: Laura Berendson
Coordinating Editor: Divya Modi

Cover designed by eStudioCalamar

Cover image designed by Pixabay

Distributed to the book trade worldwide by Springer Science+Business Media New York, 1 New York Plaza, Suite 4600, New York, NY 10004-1562, USA. Phone 1-800-SPRINGER, fax (201) 348-4505, e-mail orders-ny@springer-sbm.com, or visit www.springeronline.com. Apress Media, LLC is a California LLC and the sole member (owner) is Springer Science + Business Media Finance Inc (SSBM Finance Inc). SSBM Finance Inc is a Delaware corporation.

For information on translations, please e-mail booktranslations@springernature.com; for reprint, paperback, or audio rights, please e-mail bookpermissions@springernature.com.

Apress titles may be purchased in bulk for academic, corporate, or promotional use. eBook versions and licenses are also available for most titles. For more information, reference our Print and eBook Bulk Sales web page at http://www.apress.com/bulk-sales.

Any source code or other supplementary material referenced by the author in this book is available to readers on GitHub via the book's product page, located at www.apress.com/978-1-4842-6401-0. For more detailed information, please visit http://www.apress.com/source-code.

Printed on acid-free paper

Table of Contents

About the Author

Sagar Rahalkar is a seasoned information security professional with more than 13 years of experience in various verticals of information security. His domain expertise is mainly in AppsSec, cybercrime investigations, vulnerability assessments, penetration testing, and IT GRC. He holds a master's degree in computer science and several industry-recognized certifications such as CISM, ISO 27001LA, and ECSA. He has been closely associated with Indian law enforcement agencies for more than three years, dealing with digital crime investigations and related training, and he has received awards from senior officials of the police and defense organizations in India. He is also an author and reviewer for several publications.

About the Technical Reviewer

Parag Patil (www.linkedin.com/in/paragpatil2006) is an information security professional currently associated with Coupa Managing Security for the SaaS platform.

For more than the last 12 years, Parag has worked extensively on digital forensics, IAM, security monitoring/SecOps, security trainings, security compliance audits, vulnerability management, penetration testing, information security research, and ISMS/governance. He is the author for CIS benchmarks for AWS, Azure, and GCP.

Reviewer Acknowledgment: Thanks to my mentors (Dattatray Bhat, Yogesh Patil, Steve O'Callaghan, Shailesh Athlye, and Hans Gustavson) who have believed in me and have provided all possible opportunities to learn and grow professionally in the information security domain.

Thanks to Mahesh Navaghane, Sagar Rahalkar (author of this book), Aditi Sahasrabuddhe (my sister), Monika (my wife,) and Ira (my daughter) for their commitment toward keeping me possibly the happiest person that I have ever known.

Introduction

The number of applications is growing and so are the number of application vulnerabilities. Enterprises have shifted a lot of focus on making the applications secure. While there are a variety of solutions and products for application security, Burp Suite is really the tool of choice for many.

Burp Suite is a simple yet powerful tool used for application security testing. It is widely used for manual application security testing of not just web applications but also APIs and mobile apps. For effectively testing security of web applications, one needs to understand various web application vulnerabilities; at the same time, one also needs to have an in-depth understanding of the tools used for testing. This book helps you understand Burp Suite comprehensively, so that it can be used precisely to uncover vulnerabilities.

The book starts with basics about Burp Suite and guides you on setting up the testing environment. The following chapters cover basic building blocks of Burp Suite and take you through its various components such as the intruder, repeater, decoder, comparer, sequencer etc., in depth. In the last chapters, we will cover other useful features such as the infiltrator, collaborator, scanner, extender, and using Burp Suite for API and mobile app security testing.

CHAPTER 1

Introduction to Burp Suite

Application Security has evolved to a large extent in the last decade or so. A decade ago, finding SQL Injections in applications was easier than it is today. The applications were more prone to vulnerabilities as there were fewer defenses and less awareness among the developers. However, the situation has drastically changed today. Developers are much more aware and conscious about security, and security controls are placed throughout the Software Development Life Cycle (SDLC), making the end application comparatively secure.

Though the development processes have become more secure, today's applications are not just limited to the web. Modern applications have services and Application Programming Interfaces (API's) exposed as well as a mobile and cloud presence. This clearly increases the complexities and attack surfaces.

For an application security tester, it is vital to find all possible vulnerabilities in the entire application ecosystem.

Some Basics of Application Security

Going into details of application security and various vulnerabilities are beyond the scope of this book. In this book we will be focusing specifically on how to use the Burp Suite tool in the most efficient manner.

© Sagar Rahalkar 2021
S. Rahalkar, *A Complete Guide to Burp Suite*,
https://doi.org/10.1007/978-1-4842-6402-7_1

However, we'll quickly glance through what the common and top application vulnerabilities are. The de facto standard referred to for application vulnerabilities is OWASP. OWASP stands for Open Web Application Security Project. The last Top 10 list for web application vulnerabilities was published in 2017. The vulnerabilities are as follows:

1. **Injection** – This includes vulnerabilities that are exploited by sending untrusted input to an interpreter either as part of a query or command. Specially crafted input tricks are what the interpreter uses in executing the commands or even giving unauthorized access to data. The most common type of injection is a database injection. Other types include the Operating System (OS) command injection or LDAP Injection, etc.

2. **Broken Authentication** – This includes vulnerabilities arising out of poor implementation of authentication and session management functions. Exploiting such vulnerabilities can give attackers access to passwords, credentials, session tokens, keys, etc.

3. **Sensitive Data Exposure** – Many times, applications lack controls to protect sensitive user data like personally identifiable information (PII), health data, or even financial data. Attackers can steal such sensitive data. Lack of data encryption at rest and in transit cause most of the vulnerabilities related to sensitive data exposure.

4. **XML External Entities** – This is a special type of vulnerability wherein an attacker exploits the entity tag within the XML documents to launch several attacks like disclosing sensitive internal files, denial of service, remote code execution, etc.

5. **Broken Access Control –** Even if a user is authenticated with valid credentials, it might not be necessary to have access to all of the application. Authorization defines what an authenticated user can access. Broken authorization gives unauthorized access to the attacker to view other user accounts, sensitive files, or even modify other users' data.

6. **Security Misconfiguration –** Security misconfiguration issues are the most common in the underlying infrastructure like web servers. Insecure configurations, default credentials, unreferenced backup files, unwanted services, open cloud storage, missing security headers and cookie flags, and missing security patches all contribute to the security misconfiguration category.

7. **Cross-Site Scripting –** This is indeed the classic web application vulnerability that has been part of the OWASP list for so long. This commonly occurs when an attacker is able to inject and execute a script through an application input field. This attack can be used to hijack user sessions by stealing cookies, defacing websites, etc. Common types of cross-site scripting include Persistent, Reflected, and DOM Based.

8. **Insecure Deserialization –** Attackers can manipulate the object serialization and deserialization process to introduce malicious payloads resulting in code execution.

9. **Using Components with known Vulnerabilities –**
    It's very common for developers to import and use
    third-party code to avoid reinventing the wheel.
    However, at times the third-party code comes along
    with inherent vulnerabilities. An example is using
    the OpenSSL library, which is vulnerable to a Heart
    Bleed attack.

10. **Insufficient Logging and Monitoring –** Quite often,
    applications lack capabilities to log events that
    would help in case of an incident. In the absence of
    audit logging and detection capabilities, attackers
    can simply continue to infiltrate without getting
    detected or raising alarms.

While the OWASP Top 10 list is probably the first place to go for web
application vulnerabilities, there are many potential vulnerabilities
beyond this Top 10 list. Following are some of the strongly recommended
references in order to get a broader perspective for application security
testing:

1. **OWASP Testing Guide –** This guide is a very
    comprehensive resource covering many security
    test cases and a very handy reference guide. It is
    available at `https://owasp.org/www-project-`
    `web-security-testing-guide/assets/archive/`
    `OWASP_Testing_Guide_v4.pdf`

2. **SANS Top 25 Programming Errors –** Beyond
    the OWASP Top 10 list, SANS has published a list
    of the 25 most dangerous programming errors.
    It is available at `https://www.sans.org/top25-`
    `software-errors`

3. **OWASP API Top 10** – Application Programming
   Interfaces (API's) are very commonly used these
   days and have some unique vulnerabilities. OWASP
   has published a special API Top 10 vulnerability
   list and is available at `https://owasp.org/www-`
   `project-api-security/`

4. **OWASP Mobile Top 10** – Mobile applications have
   different sets of vulnerabilities, and some even
   vary based on the type of platform. However, the
   most common and top mobile vulnerabilities are
   available at `https://owasp.org/www-project-`
   `mobile-top-10/`

5. **OWASP IoT Top 10** – Today even household
   devices are getting smarter and connected. Such
   Internet of Things (IoT devices) are prone to many
   vulnerabilities. OWASP has published an IoT Top 10
   vulnerability list available at `https://owasp.org/`
   `www-project-internet-of-things/`

A Brief Introduction to Burp Suite

The birth of Burp Suite dates back to 2004 when Dafydd Stuttard gauged
the need for a robust web application security testing tool. In the past 16
years, the tool has evolved leaps and bounds and has added numerous
capabilities that benefit the security testing community. Burp Suite has
undoubtedly become a tool of choice for web application security testing.
Also it has evolved in a way that it can now be used to find vulnerabilities
in API's and Mobile Apps as well.

Need for Burp Suite

Today the market for application security scanning and testing tools is rapidly growing. There are so many tools available, commercial as well as free, from different vendors, supporting various technologies and features. Most of these tools are inclined toward automated scanning of software to find vulnerabilities. This is achieved either by triggering the scanner after spidering or crawling the target application or integrating the scanner directly in the DevOps cycle. While this is certainly an advantage and increases efficiency of scanning with minimum manual intervention, there are certain vulnerabilities that can be better understood and exploited through manual testing.

Manual Testing is largely dependent on two factors: the skills of the tester and the tool used for testing. A tool like Burp Suite significantly aids in fulfilling the needs of manual testing from a tooling perspective. It provides a powerful and flexible platform where the tester can efficiently find and exploit potential vulnerabilities. So, for application security scanning and testing, the best strategy would be to use a combination of both automated and manual testing. Burp Suite has excellent manual testing capabilities along with an automated scanner. So it gives the tester benefits of manual testing as well as automated scanning of vulnerabilities.

Editions

Like most of the other tools, Burp Suite comes in different forms. Different users might have different needs and one size may not fit all. Keeping in mind the varying needs of users, Burp Suite comes in three different editions.

1. **Burp Suite Community Edition** – The Burp Suite Community Edition is the most basic version, which is free to download and use. It comes with a limited set of tools and features to get started with web application security testing. If you are completely new to application security and want to explore the basics, then the Burp Suite Community Edition is certainly a very good starting point. It does have good tools and features required for basic manual web application security testing like the interception proxy, tamper and relay requests using repeater, encode and decode data, etc.

2. **Burp Suite Professional Edition** – Once you have a very good understanding of web application security and you are regularly required to test applications as part of your profession, then the Burp Suite Professional Edition is definitely recommended. The Burp Suite Professional Edition comes along with many advanced features that significantly improve your ability to find potential vulnerabilities in applications. This is the most suitable edition for individual professionals looking for excellent manual and automated security testing capabilities. Some of the advanced features include the following:

   • Testing out-of-band vulnerabilities

   • Advanced brute-force and fuzzing capabilities

   • Quickly generating exploits for CSRF, Clickjacking, etc.

- Automated scanning for vulnerabilities

- Useful extensions to further enhance vulnerability detection capabilities

More details on the Burp Suite Professional Edition can be found here - `https://portswigger.net/burp/pro`

3. **Burp Suite Enterprise Edition** – While the Burp Suite Community Edition and the Burp Suite Professional Edition were aimed at individual professionals, the Burp Suite Enterprise Edition is useful to the organizations looking for integrating security scanning in software pipelines. It doesn't have the manual testing tools as compared to the earlier editions. This edition is recommended for enterprises looking out for DevSecOps solutions.

As part of this book, we will be covering the Burp Suite Professional Edition.

Burp Suite Alternatives

We have already discussed that the market for application security scanning tools is largely growing. While Burp Suite fulfills most of the manual and automated testing needs, it is rivaled by some other tools such as those shown in Table 1-1.

Table 1-1. Scanning Tools

Commercial	Free / Open Source
Acunetix	OWASP ZAP
Netsparker	W3af
IBM AppScan	Arachni
WebInspect	Iron Wasp

More information and comparative analysis on various application security Testing tools can be found at https://www.gartner.com/reviews/market/application-security-testing

High-Level Feature Overview

The Burp Suite Professional Edition comes with a wide range of features for manual penetration testing as well as for automated scanning. Some of the useful features include the following:

1. **Manual Penetration Testing –** Intercept and tamper requests (HTTP / HTTPS), manually testing for out-of-band vulnerabilities, testing web sockets, testing token strength, easily test clickjacking and Cross-Site Request Forgery (CSRF) vulnerabilities.

2. **Advanced Automated Attacks –** Passive and active scanning to find potential vulnerabilities, advanced capabilities to brute-force and fuzz inputs.

3. **Productivity –** Detailed message analysis, efficient project options, tools to make code more readable, easy and simple vulnerability reporting.

4. **Extensions** – Burp Suite Application Store to install extensions for significantly enhancing the existing tool capabilities.

We'll be going through the above features more in detail as we proceed through the book.

Summary

We started off this chapter by explaining how application security has evolved over the last decade or so. We then glanced at some of the top web application vulnerabilities. Next we tried to understand the need for a tool like Burp Suite followed by its editions and alternatives. Finally, we concluded with a high-level overview of the features provided by Burp Suite Professional.

In the next chapter, we'll get started with installation and setup of the tool.

Exercises

- Read about the OWASP Top 10 vulnerabilities and the OWASP Testing Guide in detail.

- Read more details about the features of all the Burp Suite editions on the official website - `https://portswigger.net/`

CHAPTER 2

Setting Up the Environment

In the last chapter, we discussed some basics of application security and the need for tools like Burp Suite. In this chapter we'll get started with setting up our environment for Burp Suite.

Burp Suite Installation

Before we attempt to either install or run the Burp Suite, we need to ensure that Java is installed on the system. It is an essential prerequisite to run Burp Suite. On a Windows system, you can simply open up the command prompt and type command "java –version" to check if Java is installed, as shown in Figure 2-1.

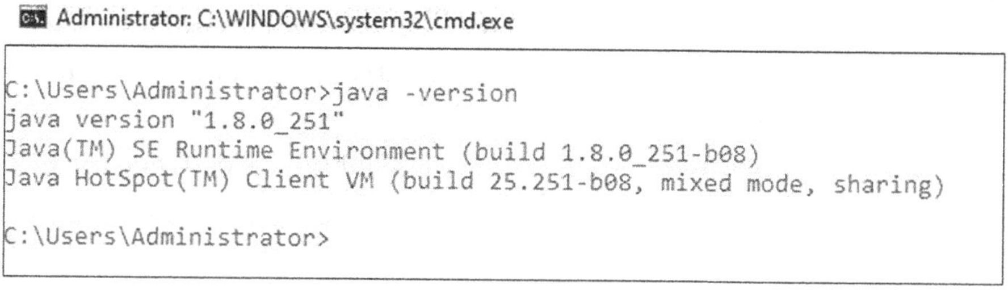

```
Administrator: C:\WINDOWS\system32\cmd.exe

C:\Users\Administrator>java -version
java version "1.8.0_251"
Java(TM) SE Runtime Environment (build 1.8.0_251-b08)
Java HotSpot(TM) Client VM (build 25.251-b08, mixed mode, sharing)

C:\Users\Administrator>
```

Figure 2-1. *Check if Java is installed*

© Sagar Rahalkar 2021
S. Rahalkar, *A Complete Guide to Burp Suite*,
https://doi.org/10.1007/978-1-4842-6402-7_2

If you don't have Java installed on your system, you can download and install Java from `https://www.oracle.com/java/technologies/javase-jre8-downloads.html`

Once we are sure that Java is installed on our system, we can now proceed with Burp Suite. We first need to download the Burp Suite from `https://portswigger.net/burp/releases/community/latest` as shown in Figure 2-2.

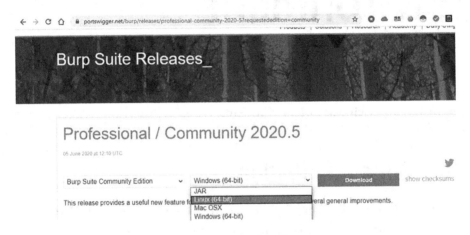

Figure 2-2. *Types of Burp Suite downloads*

You'll notice there are several forms in which you can download the Burp Suite. There are individual installers for Linux, Mac OSX, and Windows. There's also an option to download a JAR file, which can be used directly to launch Burp Suite without installing. Downloading the JAR file is the easiest way to get started. If you choose to download the installer, it is just like any other software installer and installs the Burp Suite in a few clicks. However, Java is required to be installed in both cases. Once the JAR file is downloaded, you can simply double-click it to launch the Burp Suite.

At times, while running large projects, it might happen that Burp Suite runs out of memory. To solve this problem, it is possible to launch Burp Suite by allocating a fixed amount of memory at startup. This will ensure that it doesn't run out of memory once launched. This can be done using command "java -jar -Xmx2G /path/to/burp.jar" where 2G indicates 2GB of memory. This step is completely optional. We can skip it and directly execute the JAR file to launch Burp Suite with the default configuration.

If all prerequisites are met correctly, we get a startup screen as shown in Figure 2-3.

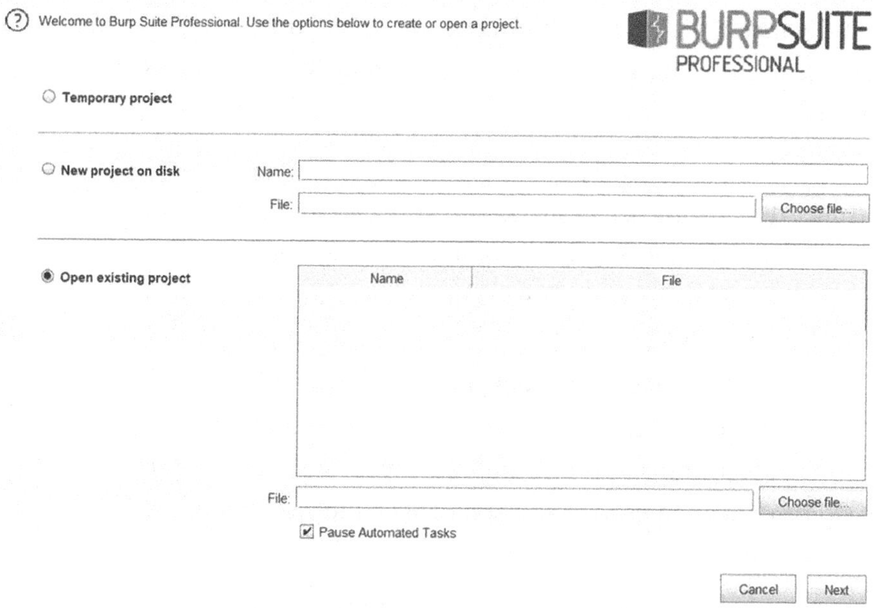

Figure 2-3. *Burp Suite Startup Screen*

Setting Up Vulnerable Target Web Application

While we set up the Burp Suite on our system, it's important to have a target application on which you will be using the tool. If you are a professional working on application security testing and penetration testing then you would be authorized to use Burp Suite on the application under the test. However, if you are just a beginner trying to get started with learning Burp Suite, then you would need to have some target application on which you could test your skills. Remember, running Burp Suite on an application on which you are not authorized can invite legal troubles. So, from a learning perspective, it's important to try your Burp Suite skills only on a test application. There are several alternatives available as shown below:

1. **Set Up OWASP Juice Shop locally** – OWASP Juice Shop is a modern web application that is deliberately made vulnerable. This can be an excellent starting point. The easiest way to get OWASP Juice Shop up and running is using its docker image. The docker image is available at `https://hub.docker.com/r/bkimminich/juice-shop`. You can simply pull the image and run it in the docker engine on any platform (Windows / Linux / MacOS).

2. **Try out online version of OWASP Juice Shop** – As a beginner, it is always recommended to set up your own copy of Juice Shop; however if you want to quickly try it out before setting it up, you can try the online version at `https://juice-shop.herokuapp.com/#/`

3. **Damn Vulnerable Web Application (DVWA) –**
   Another great application that has been made
   vulnerable intentionally for testing is DVWA. You
   can quickly set up the DVWA using docker or on a
   local web server. Detailed instructions on setting up
   and using DVWA are available at `https://github.`
   `com/ethicalhack3r/DVWA`

4. **Damn Vulnerable Web Services –** OWASP Juice
   Shop and DVWA would suffice for your learning
   needs for web application vulnerabilities.
   However, if you wish to explore more specifically
   the vulnerabilities in web services, then Damn
   Vulnerable Web Services is a good option. More
   details on setup and usage can be found at `https://`
   `github.com/snoopysecurity/dvws`

Configuring the Browser

Now that we have Burp Suite up and running, we need to configure
our browser to work along with it. First let's consider a normal scenario
without Burp Suite in the picture as shown in Figure 2-4.

Figure 2-4. *A user accessing a website directly without Burp Suite*

Referring to the image above, at a very high level and in simple terms, the following sequence of events happens:

1. The end user opens up any browser of choice.

2. The user then enters the URL of website he/she wishes to browse.

3. The browser processes the URL of the website and renders the website for the user (a series of request and response happens in the background).

Now let's consider another scenario wherein we have configured Burp Suite with the browser as shown in Figure 2-5.

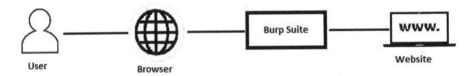

Figure 2-5. *A user accessing a website with Burp Suite*

Referring to the image above, at a very high level and in simple terms, the following sequence of events happens:

1. The end user opens up any browser of choice.

2. The user then enters the URL of the website he/she wishes to browse.

3. The browser redirects the request to Burp Suite, which then forwards the request to the target website.

4. The target website responds to the request and sends a response back to Burp Suite, which then passes on the response to be rendered in the browser.

So in this scenario, Burp Suite is acting as 'Man-in-the-Middle' between the browser and the target website. Burp Suite is able to intercept and tamper all the traffic passing through it.

We'll now see how we can configure the most popular browsers to work with Burp Suite.

Firefox

For configuring Firefox with Burp Suite:

Go to Tools ➤ Options as shown in Figure 2-6.

Figure 2-6. *Navigating the Tools ➤ Options menu in Firefox*

In the search field, enter the keyword 'network' as shown in Figure 2-7 and click on 'Settings.'

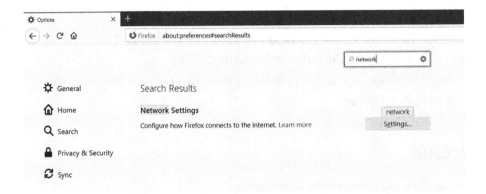

Figure 2-7. *Searching for 'Network Settings' within Firefox options*

Select 'Manual proxy configuration' as shown in Figure 2-8 and enter the IP as 127.0.0.1 (or localhost) and port as 8080.

Note: By default the Burp Suite proxy listens on port 8080. This can be customized and we'll see that in the next chapter. However, the same port number must be entered both in the browser as well as in the Burp Suite in case you wish to change the same.

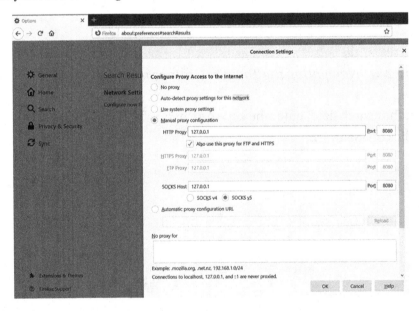

Figure 2-8. *Setting up the manual proxy configuration*

Simply click 'OK' once the proxy details have been configured.

Chrome

For configuring Chrome with Burp Suite:

Click on the three vertical dots in the right-hand corner and select 'Settings' as shown in Figure 2-9.

Figure 2-9. *Navigating to the Chrome Settings*

Search for the keyword 'proxy' as shown in Figure 2-10, and click on the 'Open your computer's proxy settings' option.

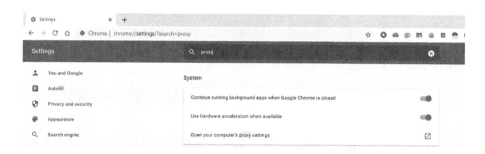

Figure 2-10. *Opening the proxy settings in Chrome*

Now enable the 'Use a proxy server' option and enter the address and port number as shown in Figure 2-11.

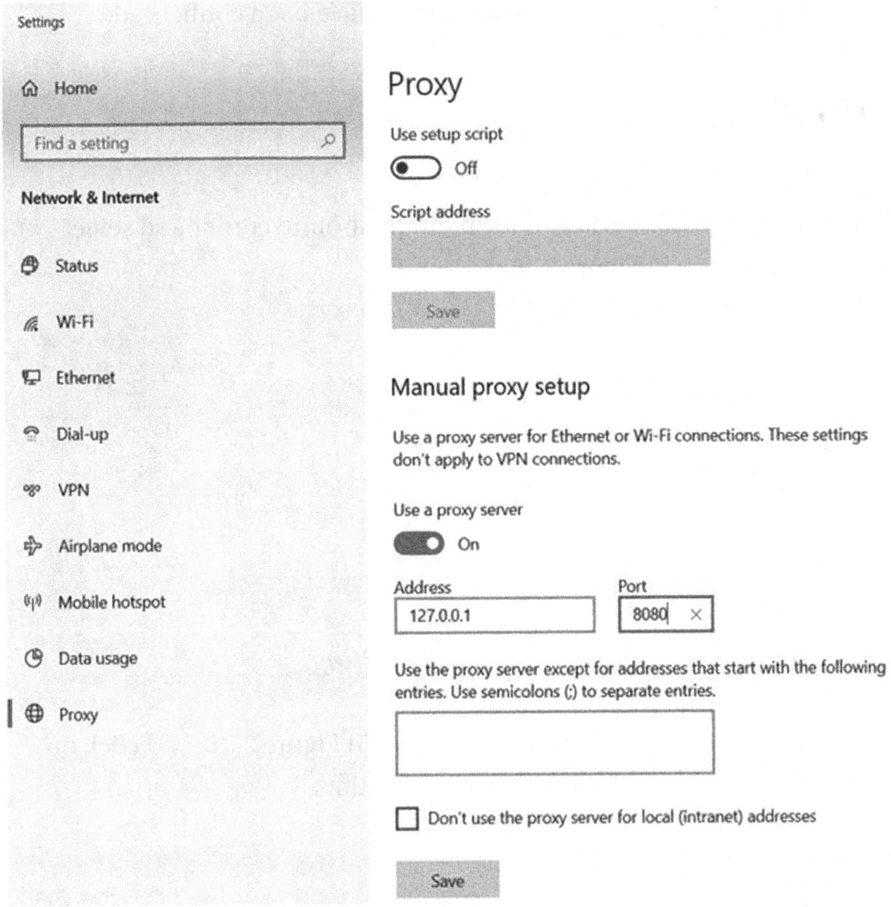

Figure 2-11. *Configuring the system proxy*

Once the proxy is configured, simply click on the 'Save' option.

Edge

For configuring Edge with Burp Suite:

Click on the three horizontal dots in the right-hand corner and select the 'Open proxy settings' as shown in Figure 2-12.

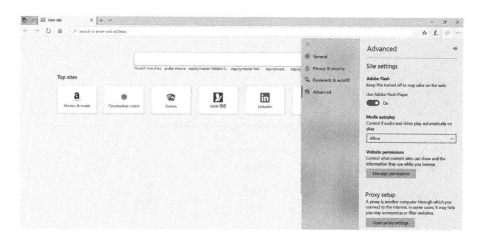

Figure 2-12. *Opening the Proxy Settings in Edge browser*

Now enable the 'Use a proxy server' option and enter the address and port number as shown in Figure 2-13.

21

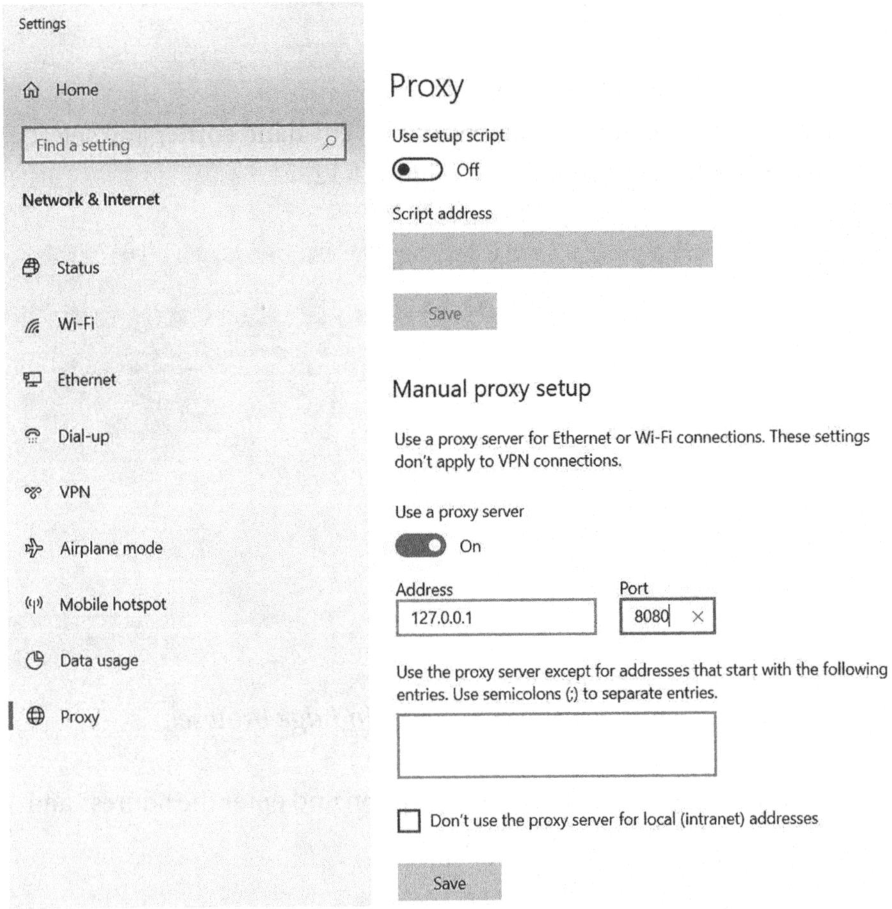

Figure 2-13.   Configuring the system proxy

Once the proxy is configured, simply click on the 'Save' option.

Opera

For configuring Opera with Burp Suite:

Click on the settings in the top right-hand corner and select the option 'Go to browser settings' as shown in Figure 2-14.

Figure 2-14. *Opening the browser settings in Opera*

In the search field, type proxy and then select the option 'Open your computer's proxy settings' as shown in Figure 2-15.

Figure 2-15. *Opening up the system proxy settings*

Now enable the 'Use a proxy server' option and enter the address and port number as shown in Figure 2-16.

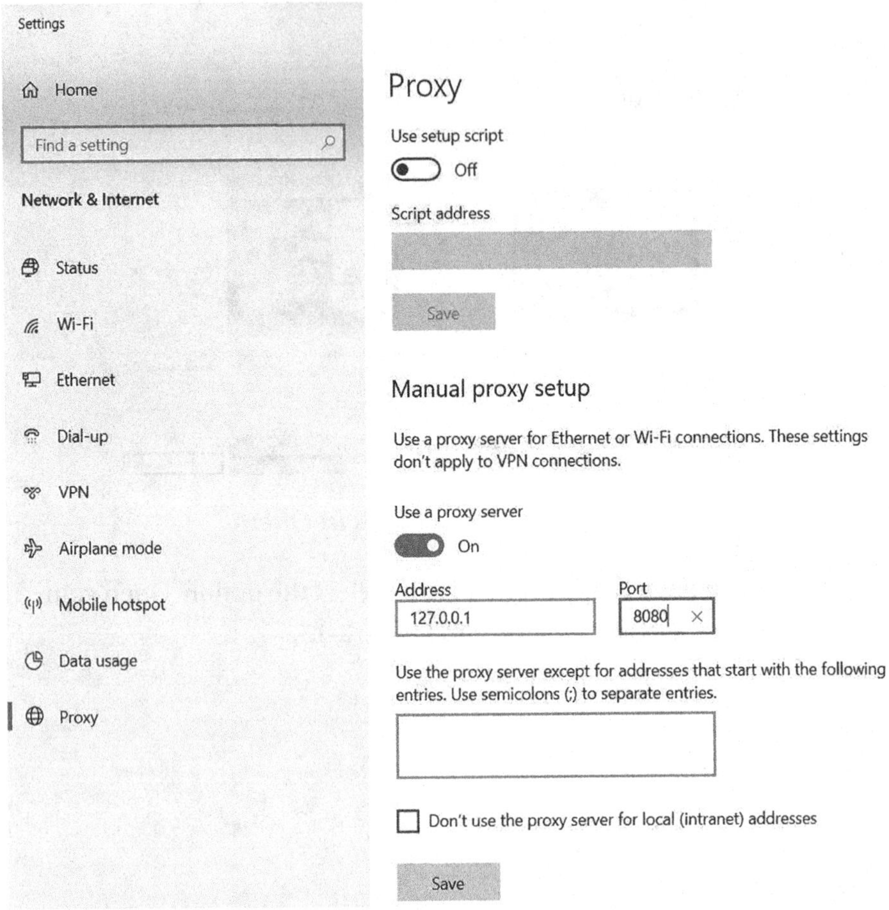

Settings

⌂ Home

Find a setting   🔍

Network & Internet

🌐 Status

📶 Wi-Fi

🖥 Ethernet

📞 Dial-up

🎛 VPN

✈ Airplane mode

((ᵢ)) Mobile hotspot

🕑 Data usage

🌐 Proxy

Proxy

Use setup script

⬤◯ Off

Script address

[   ]

[Save]

Manual proxy setup

Use a proxy server for Ethernet or Wi-Fi connections. These settings don't apply to VPN connections.

Use a proxy server

◉⬤ On

Address   Port

[127.0.0.1   ]   [8080 ×]

Use the proxy server except for addresses that start with the following entries. Use semicolons (;) to separate entries.

[   ]

☐ Don't use the proxy server for local (intranet) addresses

[Save]

Figure 2-16. *Configuring the system proxy*

Once the proxy is configured, simply click on the 'Save' option.

So far we have seen how to configure browsers like Firefox, Chrome, Edge, and Opera to work along with Burp Suite. It simply requires configuring the network proxy option. However, it is important to note that once the browser proxy is configured, all the traffic initiating from the browser will compulsorily pass through Burp Suite. If you are working on multiple tabs within a browser and testing an application in one tab while accessing email in another, all this traffic will be routed through Burp Suite. In case you with to pass only selective traffic through Burp Suite, you need to make use of additional browser plugins such as those shown in Table 2-1.

Table 2-1. *Additional Browser Plugins for Proxy*

Firefox	Proxy SwitchyOmega, FoxyProxy
Chrome	Proxy SwitchyOmega, FoxyProxy
Edge	N/A
Opera	Proxy Switcher & Manager

The above plugins are simple to use and allow custom selective traffic to pass through Burp Suite. Using these plugins is completely optional. If you don't wish to use these plugins, you can simply use two separate instances of browser, one for application testing and the other for personal use. Or it is also possible to scope out only the required traffic in Burp Suite that we will be learning in an upcoming chapter.

Summary

In this chapter we saw how to download, install, and get started with the Burp Suite tool. We then explored various options available for setting up vulnerable targets to practice Burp Suite skills. We also learned how to configure different browsers to work along with the Burp Suite.

In the next chapter, we'll see how to configure some of the basic settings in the Burp Suite like the Proxy, User Options, and Project Options.

Exercises

- Download the latest version of the Burp Suite.

- Try to launch Burp Suite from the command line, allocating custom memory size.

- Try and explore how to use the FoxyProxy plugin for Firefox and Chrome.

CHAPTER 3

Proxy, User Options, and Project Options

In the last chapter, we saw some basics of Burp Suite installation, setting up the vulnerable application and configuring different browsers to work along. In this chapter, we'll get started with some basics of Burp Suite proxy along with several user and project options.

Proxy

Proxy is really the essence of Burp Suite. Leveraging the proxy functionality, Burp Suite is able to see all the traffic passing through it. In the previous chapters, we have already seen how Burp Suite works as Man-in-the-Middle and helps us intercept requests.

In order to make Burp Suite functional, we have to have a complete configuration at two different ends. One part is configuring the network proxy in the browser that we saw in the previous chapter. Another part is ensuring the Burp Suite proxy is configured properly. By default, when we start the Burp Suite, its proxy listens on port 8080. In this case you don't need to do any more configurations. However, if port 8080 is already being used by some other application on your system, then there would be a port conflict and the Burp Suite proxy service would fail to start. In this case you can start the Burp Suite proxy listener on any other custom port that is not already in use. To do this, navigate to the Proxy tab as shown in Figure 3-1.

© Sagar Rahalkar 2021
S. Rahalkar, *A Complete Guide to Burp Suite*,
https://doi.org/10.1007/978-1-4842-6402-7_3

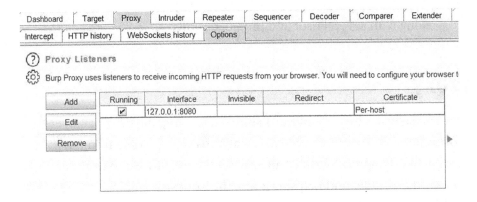

| Dashboard | Target | Proxy | Intruder | Repeater | Sequencer |

| Intercept | HTTP history | WebSockets history | Options |

| Forward | Drop | Intercept is off | Action |

| Raw | Hex | Hackvertor |

Figure 3-1. *Proxy Option in the Burp Suite*

Then go to the 'Options' tab as shown in Figure 3-2. You'll notice that the Burp Suite proxy is running by default on localhost and port 8080.

| Dashboard | Target | Proxy | Intruder | Repeater | Sequencer | Decoder | Comparer | Extender |

| Intercept | HTTP history | WebSockets history | Options |

(?) **Proxy Listeners**

{⚙} Burp Proxy uses listeners to receive incoming HTTP requests from your browser. You will need to configure your browser t

	Running	Interface	Invisible	Redirect	Certificate
Add	✔	127.0.0.1:8080			Per-host
Edit					
Remove					

Figure 3-2. *Proxy options*

To enable the Burp Suite proxy on the custom port, click the 'Add' button as shown in Figure 3-3.

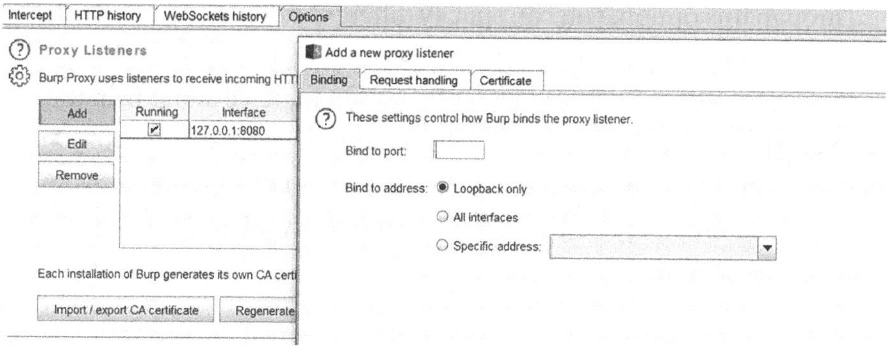

Figure 3-3. *Adding new proxy listener*

Now you can bind the Burp Suite proxy to any custom port. After configuring the custom port, you can leave the bind address to default as 'Loopback only' or if there are multiple network interfaces on your system, you can select any one of them using the drop-down menu in the "Specific address" option.

Once the Burp Suite proxy is configured, we are all set to intercept application requests. By default, the Burp Suite will intercept only requests. In any particular scenario, if you are required to intercept responses as well, then it can be done through additional configuration. To enable interception of responses, go to Proxy ➤ Options and check the option "Intercept responses based on the following rules:" as shown in Figure 3-4.

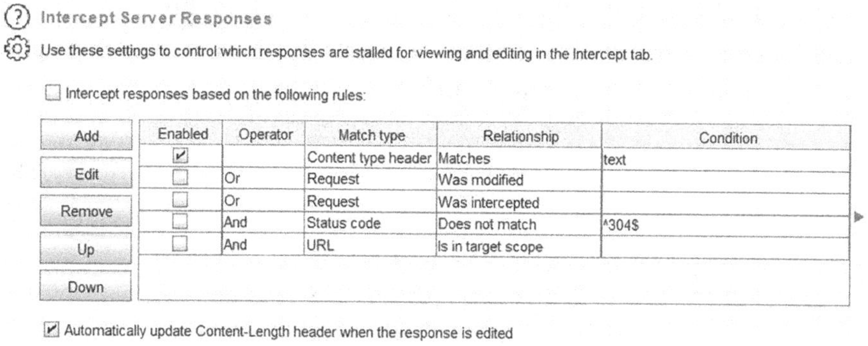

Figure 3-4. *Intercepting server responses*

Through this option, you can specify different rules based on which the Burp Suite proxy would intercept responses.

Now that we have the browser configuration in place along with the Burp Suite proxy, we can try to intercept a request. Navigate to "Proxy ➤ Intercept" and Click on "Intercept if off" (to turn on the intercept). Now in the browser enter any URL and observe the proxy tab in Burp Suite as shown in Figure 3-5.

Figure 3-5. *Intercepting HTTP request*

You will notice the request you made from the browser is trapped in Burp Suite. You can now click on Forward if you want to allow rendering the URL in the browser. You can drop the request and the browser won't load the URL. If you turn off the Intercept option, then all requests and responses will be captured in Burp Suite without any manual intervention. The right-hand corner also gives an option to give a color to the request if you want to highlight it for some reason along with comments.

The HTTP History tab shows all the requests that have passed through Burp Suite so far as shown in Figure 3-6.

Figure 3-6. *HTTP Proxy History*

The proxy history captures important information like host, method, URL, parameters (if any), status on whether the request was edited/tampered, HTTP Status code, Content Length, MIME Type, Extensions, Title, IP, cookies, and time of the request. This is really a wealth of information to start with. Burp Suite is also capable of capturing Web Socket traffic by default and it can be seen in the Web Sockets history tab.

Burp Suite CA Certificate

We have already seen in the previous chapter that Burp Suite proxy works as Man-in-the-Middle. While accessing an application over HTTPS through Burp Suite, the proxy will generate a TLS certificate signed by its certificate authority and store it on the client system. To use Burp Suite most efficiently in case of HTTPS, it is advisable to download and install the Burp Suite CA Certificate as trusted in the browser.

To import and install the Burp Suite CA certificate, first ensure your Firefox browser is configured to work along with the Burp Suite proxy. Then in the address bar, type URL "`http://burpsuite`" as shown in Figure 3-7.

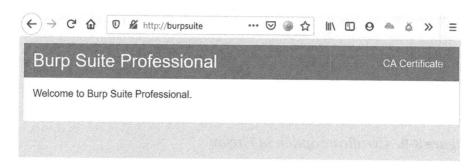

Figure 3-7. *Burp Suite CA Certificate*

Notice the right-hand corner for "CA Certificate." Click on that option to and download the file "cacert.der" as shown in Figure 3-8.

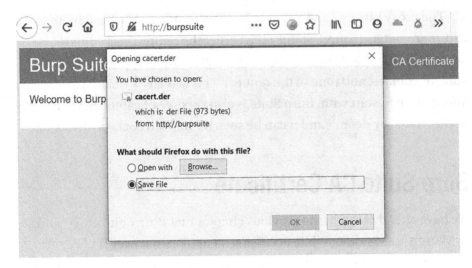

Figure 3-8. Downloading the Burp Suite CA Certificate

Next, go to Firefox Tools ➤ Options and type 'cert' in the search bar as shown in Figure 3-9.

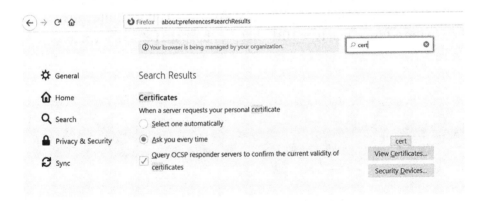

Figure 3-9. Certificate option in Firefox

Click on the option 'View Certificates' and then use the 'Import' button as shown in Figure 3-10 to select the Burp Suite Certificate that we previously downloaded.

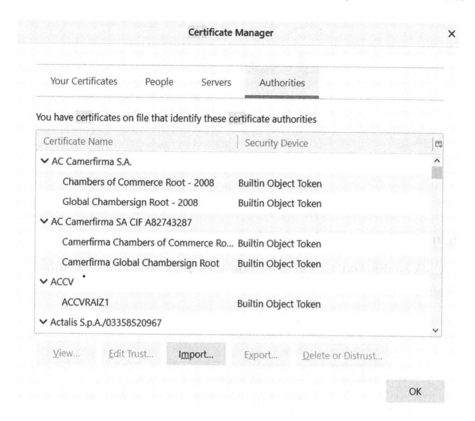

Figure 3-10. *Firefox Certificate Manager*

Platform Authentication, Upstream Proxy Servers, SOCKS Proxy

Platform Authentication

There are certain scenarios where the application hosted on the target web server is protected by authentication. In such a case, we need to configure the credentials in Burp Suite. In the absence of credentials, Burp Suite won't be able to access the protected portion of the application and miss out on potential checks. To configure platform authentication, navigate to "User Options ➤ Connections ➤ Platform Authentication" as shown in Figure 3-11.

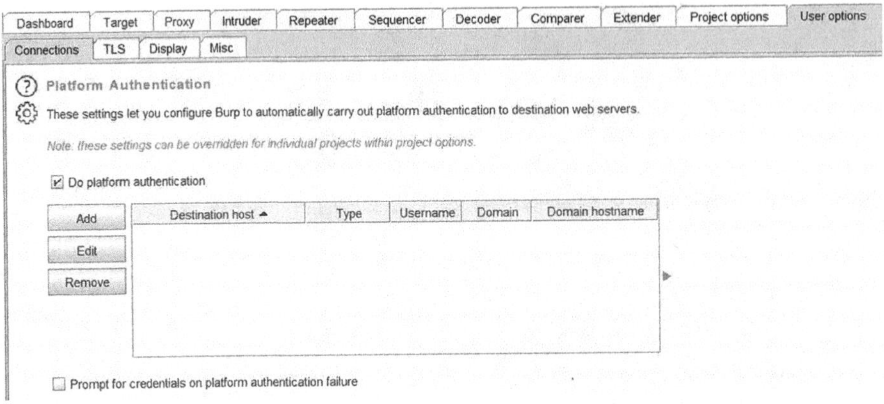

| Dashboard | Target | Proxy | Intruder | Repeater | Sequencer | Decoder | Comparer | Extender | Project options | User options |

| Connections | TLS | Display | Misc |

(?) Platform Authentication

{O} These settings let you configure Burp to automatically carry out platform authentication to destination web servers.

Note: these settings can be overridden for individual projects within project options.

[✓] Do platform authentication

| Add | | Destination host ▲ | Type | Username | Domain | Domain hostname |
| Edit |
| Remove |

[ ] Prompt for credentials on platform authentication failure

Figure 3-11. *Configuring the Platform Authentication*

Click on the 'Add' button and a pop-up window will appear as shown in Figure 3-12.

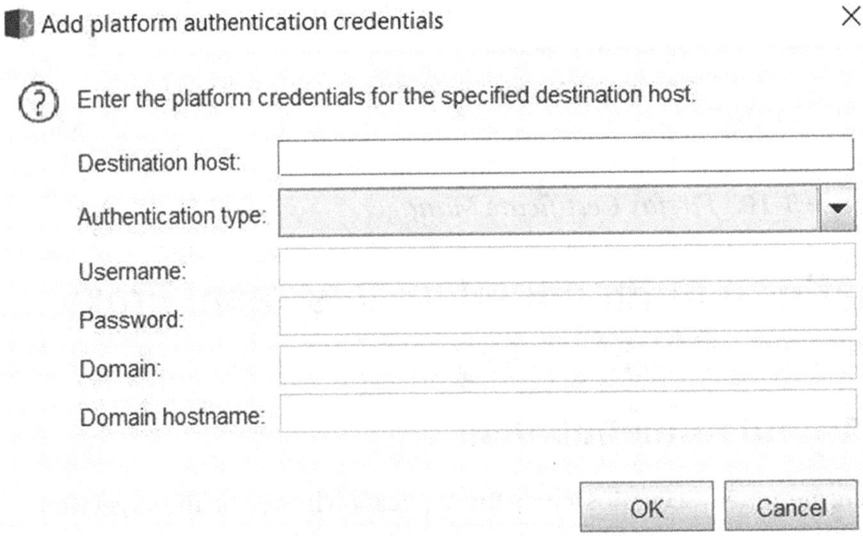

■ Add platform authentication credentials   ✕

(?) Enter the platform credentials for the specified destination host.

Destination host: [   ]

Authentication type: [▼]

Username: [   ]

Password: [   ]

Domain: [   ]

Domain hostname: [   ]

[OK]   [Cancel]

Figure 3-12. *Setting up the Platform Authentication*

We need to configure the destination host either in the form of an IP address or hostname, authentication type either of Basic, NTLM V2, NTLM V1, Digest, Username and Password, and the Domain if applicable. Once these settings are recorded, Burp Suite can seamlessly access the protected part of the application with the help of these credentials.

Upstream Proxy Servers

While testing applications in certain network environments, it may happen that there's no direct access to that target application. In such a case, we might need to connect to a proxy server first and then connect to the target application. Burp Suite allows easy configuration of upstream proxy servers. Simply navigate to "User Options ➤ Connections ➤ Upstream Proxy Servers" as shown in Figure 3-13.

Figure 3-13. *Configuring the Upstream Proxy Servers*

Click on the 'Add' button as shown in Figure 3-14, and configure the required proxy settings.

35

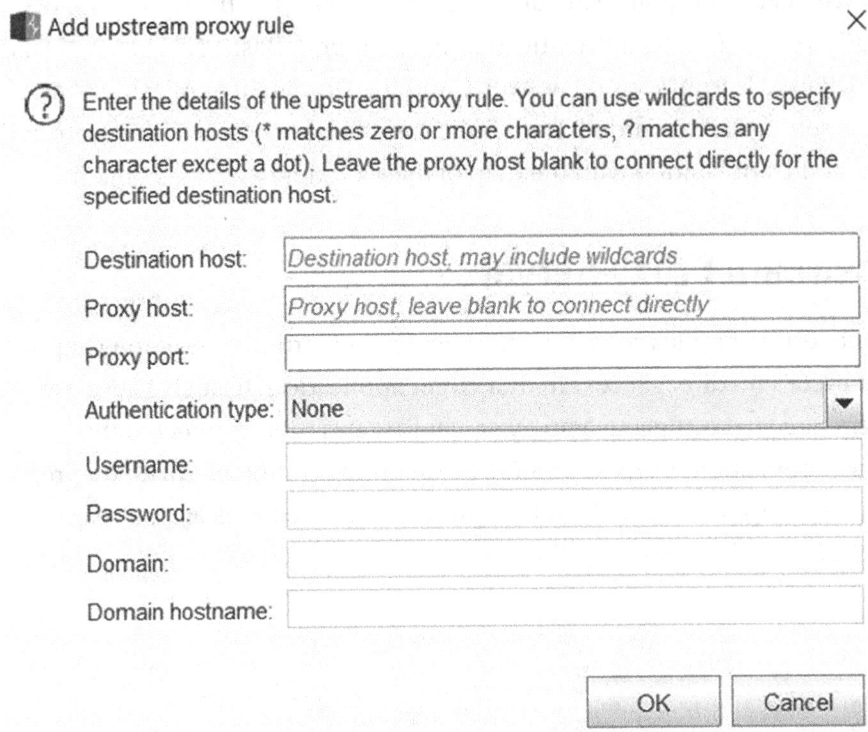

Add upstream proxy rule   ×

(?)   Enter the details of the upstream proxy rule. You can use wildcards to specify
      destination hosts (* matches zero or more characters, ? matches any
      character except a dot). Leave the proxy host blank to connect directly for the
      specified destination host.

Destination host: Destination host, may include wildcards

Proxy host: Proxy host, leave blank to connect directly

Proxy port:

Authentication type: None   ▼

Username:

Password:

Domain:

Domain hostname:

OK   Cancel

Figure 3-14. *Adding the upstream proxy rule*

SOCKS Proxy

Burp Suite also allows you to make all connection requests through a
SOCKS proxy. To configure Burp Suite with SOCKS Proxy, navigate to
"User Options ➤ Connections ➤ SOCKS Proxy" as shown in Figure 3-15,
and configure the required proxy settings.

(?) SOCKS Proxy

{⚙} These settings let you configure Burp to use a SOCKS proxy. This setting is applied at the TCP level, and all outbound requests will be sent via this proxy. proxy configured here.

Note: these settings can be overridden for individual projects within project options.

☐ Use SOCKS proxy

SOCKS proxy host: [   ]
SOCKS proxy port: [   ]
Username: [   ]
Password: [   ]

☐ Do DNS lookups over SOCKS proxy

Figure 3-15. *Adding SOCKS proxy*

Hotkeys

The Burp Suite tool has many tabs, tools, and options that we can work with. We'll be discussing them in detail in upcoming chapters. At first, the Burp Suite tools and tabs might seem overwhelming. But they all get familiar as you start using them. While all these tools and tabs can be accessed with the click of a button, at times while working on projects, it is much easier to use keyboard shortcuts than using mouse clicks.

The Burp Suite tool offers configuration of Hotkeys, which are nothing but the keyboard shortcuts to access certain tools or tabs. To configure Hotkeys, navigate to User Options ➤ Misc ➤ Hotkeys as shown in Figure 3-16.

Dashboard	Target	Proxy	Intruder	Repeater	Sequencer	Decoder	Comparer	Extender	Project options	User options

Connections	TLS	Display	Misc

(?) Hotkeys

{⚙} These settings let you configure hotkeys for common actions. These include item-specific actions such as "Send to Repeater", global actions such as "Switch to

Action	Hotkey
Send to Repeater	Ctrl+R
Send to Intruder	Ctrl+I
Send to Comparer	
Send request to Comparer	
Send response to Comparer	
Send to Decoder	
Send to Sequencer	

[Edit hotkeys]

Figure 3-16. *Configuring the Burp Suite Hotkeys*

37

By default, Hotkeys for common functionalities within the Burp Suite are already configured. However there's an option 'Edit hotkeys' either to change the default hotkeys or configure hotkeys for additional functionalities.

The Table 3-1 lists some of the common default hotkeys.

Table 3-1. *Default Hotkeys in Burp Suite*

Hotkey	Purpose
Ctrl + R	Send to Repeater
Ctrl + I	Send to Intruder
Ctrl + F	Forward intercepted proxy message
Ctrl + Shift + T	Switch to Target
Ctrl + Shift + P	Switch to Proxy
Ctrl + Shift + I	Switch to Intruder
Ctrl + Shift + R	Switch to Repeater
Ctrl + Shift + O	Switch to Project Options
Ctrl + Shift + U	URL Decode
Ctrl + Shift + B	Base-64 Decode
Ctrl + B	Base-64 Encode

Apart from the hotkeys in the above table, all other standard keyboard shortcuts for selecting all text, cut, copy, and paste work in the standard way.

Project Backups

While working on projects using Burp Suite, large amounts of data in the form of requests and responses get generated. It becomes necessary to save a copy of this data at regular intervals. Instead of doing this task manually, Burp Suite offers a feature to take a backup of data automatically after specified intervals.

To enable automatic backups, navigate to User Options ➤ Misc ➤ Automatic Project Backup as shown in Figure 3-17.

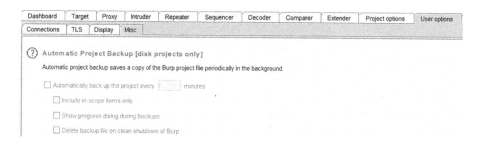

Figure 3-17. *Configuring automatic project backups*

Using this feature, we can specify the duration in minutes after which Burp Suite will automatically trigger the backup.

Rest API

While we use the Burp Suite mostly for manual application security testing, there could be so many other tools and use cases that need to work along with the Burp Suite. There could be other security tools that need to integrate with Burp Suite or certain custom automation scenarios as well that need to automatically trigger actions in Burp Suite.

For all such purposes, Burp Suite provides users with a REST API interface. REST stands for Representational State Transfer and API stands for Application Programming Interface. REST API is the most popular way of interconnecting different applications.

To enable the Burp Suite REST API, go to "User Options ➤ Misc" as shown in Figure 3-18.

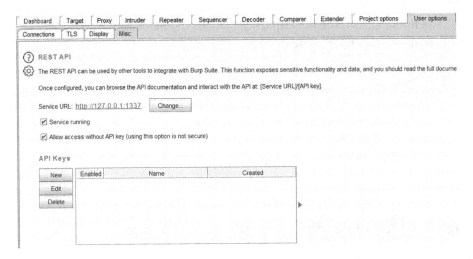

Figure 3-18. *Setting up the Burp Suite REST API interface*

To enable the Burp Suite REST API, simply check the option "Service running." The REST API will be available by default on http://127.0.0.1:1337 as shown in Figure 3-19.

Figure 3-19. *The Burp Suite REST API Interface*

The REST API interface lists all the verbs or methods supported, the endpoints to be called, the parameters to be passed, and the expected responses. Now it completely depends on a particular scenario or use case on how this REST API interface can be utilized.

Performance Feedback

As like with any other tool, Burp Suite has a provision to capture and send certain diagnostic data that could be useful in improving Burp Suite's performance. This is a completely optional feature, and if enabled it only collects data about internal functioning and not about specific users or project data. Burp Suite also provides features to log all exceptions or to report a specific bug to the Burp Suite team.

To use Performance Feedback options, navigate to User Options ➤ Misc ➤ Performance Feedback as shown in Figure 3-20.

Figure 3-20. *Configuring the performance feedback*

Project Options

These options include Hostname resolution, Out-of-Scope Requests, Redirections, TLS Configuration, Session Handling Rules, Cookie Jar. and Macros.

41

Timeouts

Handling requests and responses is the core functionality of Burp Suite. There could be scenarios like the target application is down, or there are connectivity issues wherein Burp Suite needs to decide how long it should wait for a response for a request before dropping it off. These settings are defined by the timeout values. They are configured by default and can be left untouched unless there's an explicit need to change the timeout values. For changing the default timeout values, navigate to "Project Options ➤ Connections ➤ Time Outs" as shown in Figure 3-21.

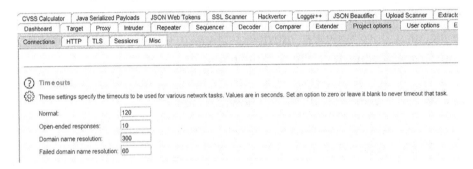

Figure 3-21. *Configuring the request timeouts*

Hostname Resolutions

Hostname resolution usually happens with the help of either the local host file or the network DNS. However, Burp Suite allows for custom hostname resolutions. This might be useful in particular scenarios where an application hosted on an intranet needs to be accessed using a specific hostname or URL.

To define custom hostname resolution rules, navigate to "Project Options ➤ Connections ➤ Hostname Resolutions" as shown in Figure 3-22.

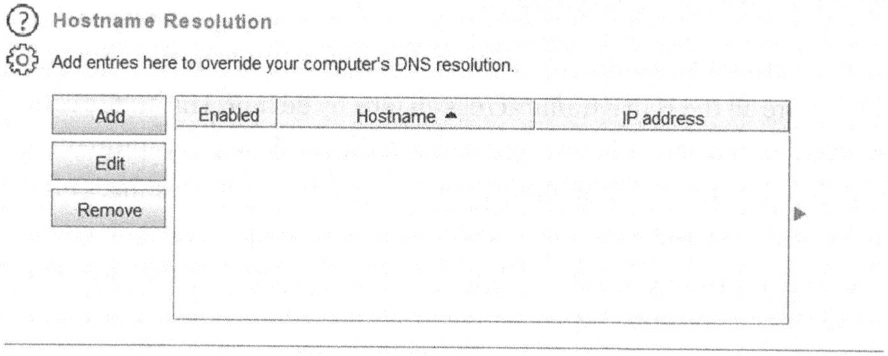

(?) Hostname Resolution

{O} Add entries here to override your computer's DNS resolution.

Add	Enabled	Hostname ▲	IP address
Edit			
Remove			▶

Figure 3-22. *Configuring the hostname resolution*

Click on the 'Add' button and then you'll get a pop-up window to enter a custom Hostname and associated IP address as shown in Figure 3-23.

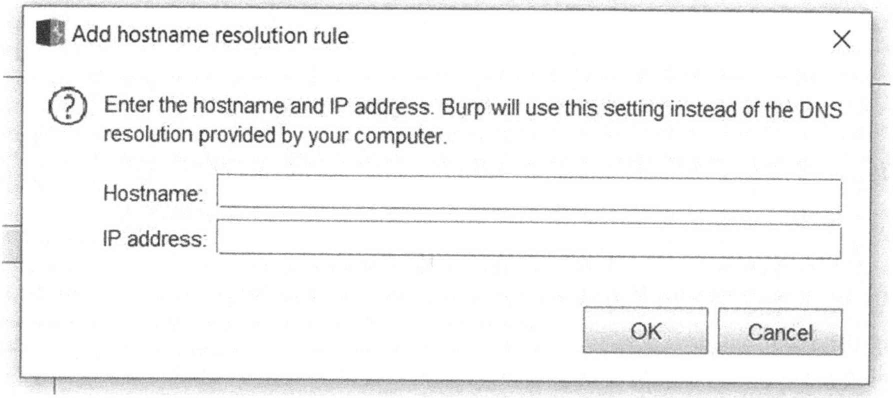

■ Add hostname resolution rule   ✕

(?) Enter the hostname and IP address. Burp will use this setting instead of the DNS
     resolution provided by your computer.

Hostname: [   ]

IP address: [   ]

                                          OK   Cancel

Figure 3-23. *Adding the hostname resolution rule*

Out-of-Scope Requests

Once the browser is configured to work along with Burp Suite, Burp Suite will capture all the HTTP traffic across all tabs by default. This traffic can be overwhelming and distracting. Out of all the traffic that is captured, we need to concentrate only on the required target that we are testing. This can be achieved using a scope that we will be covering in a later chapter. Burp Suite provides a feature to simply drop all the requests that are out of scope. This can be done by navigating to "Project Options ➤ Connections ➤ Out-of-scope Requests" as shown in Figure 3-24.

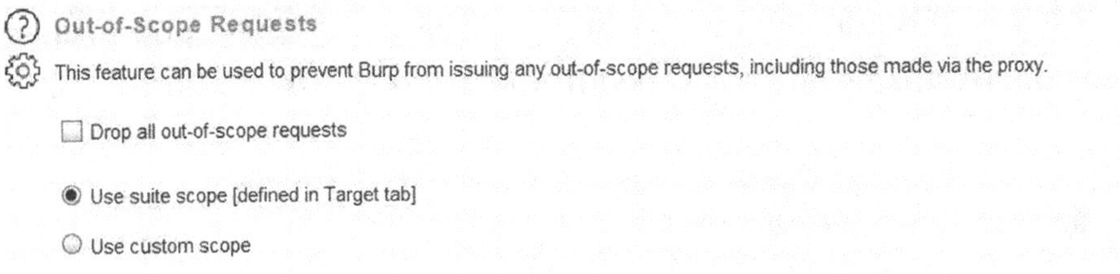

Figure 3-24. Configuring the rules for Out-of-Scope requests

Selecting the "Use custom scope" option we can explicitly add URLs that we wish to exclude from the scope and drop off the proxy as shown in Figure 3-25.

(?) Out-of-Scope Requests

{○} This feature can be used to prevent Burp from issuing any out-of-scope requests, including those made via the proxy.

☐ Drop all out-of-scope requests

○ Use suite scope [defined in Target tab]

◉ Use custom scope

☐ Use advanced scope control

Include in scope

Add	Enabled	Prefix
Edit		
Remove		
Paste URL		
Load ...		

Exclude from scope

Add	Enabled	Prefix
Edit		
Remove		
Paste URL		
Load ...		

Figure 3-25. *Defining rules for Out-of-Scope requests*

Redirections

Automated application scanning requires processing of HTTP redirections.
The scan engine has to take action once it detects any page redirection.
Burp Suite has redirection rules configured by default and those can be
left untouched unless there's an explicit need to change them, or there's
a need for additional configuration of JavaScript-driven redirections. For
configuring redirection rules, navigate to "Project Options ➤ HTTP ➤
Redirections" as shown in Figure 3-26.

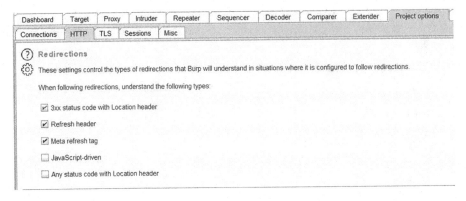

Figure 3-26. *Configuring the redirections*

Cookie Jar

Any application scanning / testing tool needs to maintain a repository of cookies that it will use to manage the ongoing application sessions. The in-session detection capability is specifically required when performing automated scanning. Burp Suite stores the application cookies in a container called "Cookie Jar." By default the Cookie Jar monitors the Proxy traffic to extract and store any cookies; however, we can explicitly instruct Burp Suite to monitor and capture cookies out of other tools like Scanner, Repeater, Intruder, Sequencer, and Extender. This can be done by navigating to "Project Options ➤ Sessions ➤ Cookie Jar" as shown in Figure 3-27.

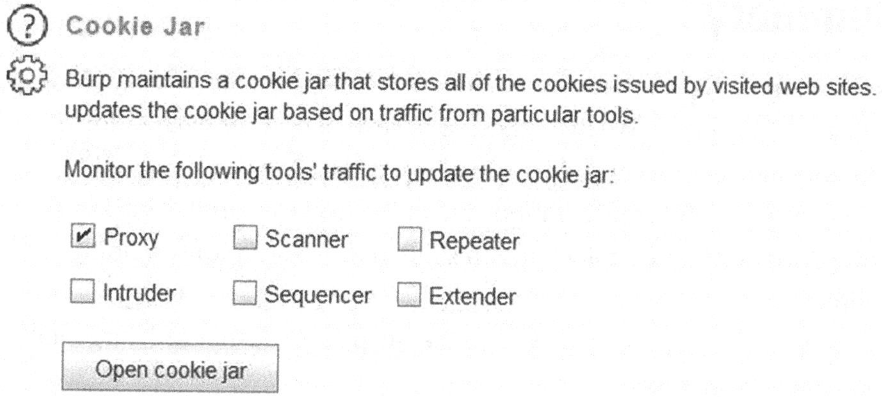

(?) Cookie Jar

{☼} Burp maintains a cookie jar that stores all of the cookies issued by visited web sites.
updates the cookie jar based on traffic from particular tools.

Monitor the following tools' traffic to update the cookie jar:

☑ Proxy   ☐ Scanner   ☐ Repeater

☐ Intruder   ☐ Sequencer   ☐ Extender

    Open cookie jar

Figure 3-27. Configuring the Cookie Jar options

Macros

In the process of application security testing, it may be required to perform
a certain sequence of actions repeatedly. Burp Suite provides an excellent
functionality of macros to achieve this. The macro editor is available at
"Project Options ➤ Sessions ➤ Macros" as shown in Figure 3-28. You can
simply click on the 'Add' button and follow the wizard to record steps.

Figure 3-28. Configuring the macros

Summary

In this chapter we learned about configuring the Burp Suite proxy along with a CA Certificate. We then glanced at several options like platform authentication, upstream proxy, socks proxy, etc. Next we explored several other useful configurations including hotkeys, project backups, using Burp Suite API, project options, hostname resolutions, scoping, and redirections.

In the next chapter we'll explore the Burp Suite dashboard, target tab, and engagement tools.

Exercises

- Configure your favorite browser and Burp Suite to work on a custom proxy port.

- Try to install Burp Suite CA Certificate for Chrome, Edge and Opera.

- Go through the default Hotkey list and try to configure additional shortcuts of your choice.

CHAPTER 4

Dashboard, Target, and Engagement Tools

In the last chapter, we saw some basics about configuring the proxy, user options, and project options. In this chapter we'll get started with getting familiar with the Burp Suite dashboard, target, and engagement tools.

Dashboard

Dashboard, as the name suggests, is that important part of Burp Suite that essentially summarizes different activities and tasks that are running across components. Figure 4-1 shows a typical view of the Burp Suite dashboard.

© Sagar Rahalkar 2021
S. Rahalkar, *A Complete Guide to Burp Suite*,
https://doi.org/10.1007/978-1-4842-6402-7_4

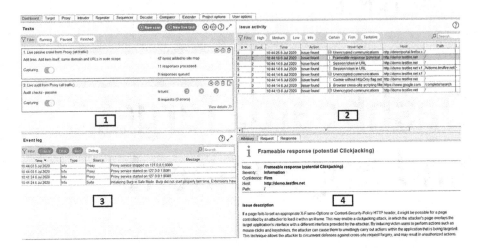

Figure 4-1. *The Burp Suite Dashboard*

For better understanding, we'll divide the dashboard into four parts and try to explain each in detail. For learning purposes, refer to the numbers from 1 to 4 in Figure 4-1.

The first part of the dashboard shows data around the ongoing scans as shown in Figure 4-2. The scans can be either passive or active. If there are multiple scans running, then we can filter them based on their state: running, paused, or finished. We also get to see a high-level summary of issues found in the scans. There's also an option to create a new scan task, which we will be exploring separately in an upcoming chapter.

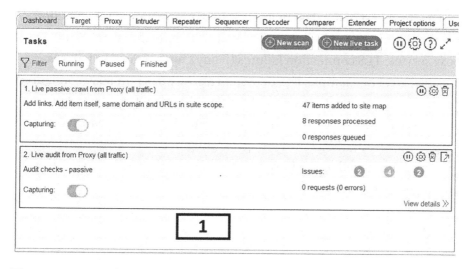

Figure 4-2. *Tasks in the Burp Suite Dashboard*

The second part of the dashboard is as shown in Figure 4-3. It might happen that either a passive scan or an active scan is running, and in either case the list of vulnerabilities found is highlighted in this section. This section also highlights information like time when the issue was found, the issue type, the host or target on which the issue was found, the vulnerable URL Path, severity of the issue, and the confidence level. Burp Suite may flag different confidence levels for different issues based on the responses; however, the issues need manual verification to ascertain their validity.

# ▾	Task	Time	Action	Issue type	Host	Path	L	Severity	Confidence	Comment
8	2	10:44:25 6 Jul 2020	Issue found	Unencrypted communications	http://detectportal.firefox.c	/		Low	Certain	
7	2	10:44:16 6 Jul 2020	Issue found	Frameable response (potential	http://demo.testfire.net	/		Information	Firm	
6	2	10:44:14 6 Jul 2020	Issue found	Session token in URL	http://demo.testfire.net	/		Medium	Firm	
5	2	10:44:14 6 Jul 2020	Issue found	Session token in URL	http://demo.testfire.net.x f../h/demo.testfire.net/			Medium	Firm	
4	2	10:44:14 6 Jul 2020	Issue found	Unencrypted communications	http://demo.testfire.net.x f	/		Low	Certain	
3	2	10:44:14 6 Jul 2020	Issue found	Cookie without HttpOnly flag set	http://demo.testfire.net	/		Low	Firm	
2	2	10:44:14 6 Jul 2020	Issue found	Browser cross-site scripting filte	https://www.google.com	/complete/search		Information	Certain	
1	2	10:44:13 6 Jul 2020	Issue found	Unencrypted communications	http://demo.testfire.net	/		Low	Certain	

Figure 4-3. *Issue activity in the Burp Suite Dashboard*

The third part of the dashboard summarizes the Burp Suite functional events as shown in Figure 4-4. These mainly include the status of the proxy service, TLS connection failures (if any), authentication failures, timeouts, etc. For example, if your system already has port 8080 configured with some other service, this part of the dashboard will highlight that proxy service couldn't be started on port 8080. Or if for any reason the proxy service stops, then it will also get highlighted here. Overall, it gives a picture about whether the Burp Suite proxy and related services are running properly or not.

Event log

Time ▼	Type	Source	Message
10:44:03 6 Jul 2020	Info	Proxy	Proxy service stopped on 127.0.0.1:8080
10:44:03 6 Jul 2020	Info	Proxy	Proxy service started on 127.0.0.1:8081
10:41:24 6 Jul 2020	Info	Proxy	Proxy service started on 127.0.0.1:8080
10:41:24 6 Jul 2020	Info	Suite	Initializing Burp in Safe Mode. Burp did not start properly last time. Extensions have not been loaded and som

Figure 4-4. The event log in the Burp Suite Dashboard

The last part of the dashboard as shown in Figure 4-5 highlights issue details. If you wish to see details of any of the issues highlighted during the passive or active scan, then simply click that issue as shown in Figure 4-3 and details will be available accordingly. The issue details include the complete issue description and remediation recommendation, along with the actual request and response.

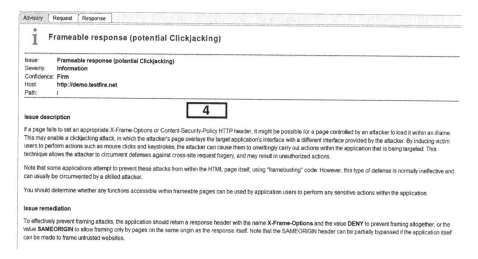

Figure 4-5. *Issue details in the Burp Suite Dashboard*

Target Tab

Like the Burp Suite dashboard that we saw in the previous section, the Target tab is an equally important work area. The target tab again has multiple panes as shown in Figure 4-6.

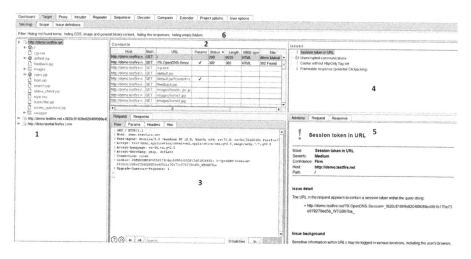

Figure 4-6. *Target tab in Burp Suite*

53

To understand different parts of the target tab, let's take one part at a time referring to the numbers 1 to 6 as per Figure 4-6.

The leftmost section in the target tab numbers as '1' in Figure 4-6 is shown in Figure 4-7. This section creates the hierarchy of the site that we are browsing through. It lists all the leaf nodes, folders, etc., in the form of a well-defined tree structure. This helps in getting an idea about how big the site / application could be or what its contents are in common. It is very similar to a sitemap.

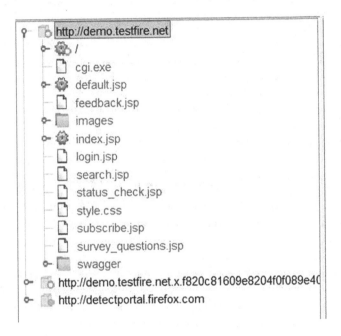

Figure 4-7. *Application map / hierarchy*

The next section numbered as '2' as per Figure 4-6 is shown in Figure 4-8. This section lists down all the HTTP requests that were made along with other details like the exact host, HTTP method used, target URL, if the URL had any parameters, HTTP status response code, content length, MIME type, and the title of the page, if any. Simply going through this section can help you find interesting URLs especially those having parameters to inject.

Host	Meth..	URL	Params	Status ▲	Length	MIME type	Title
http://demo.testfire.n...	GET	/		200	9635	HTML	Altoro Mutual ▲
http://demo.testfire.n...	GET	/?X-OpenDNS-Sessi...	✓	302	365	HTML	302 Found
http://demo.testfire.n...	GET	/cgi.exe					
http://demo.testfire.n...	GET	/default.jsp					
http://demo.testfire.n...	GET	/default.jsp?content=s.	✓				
http://demo.testfire.n...	GET	/feedback.jsp					
http://demo.testfire.n...	GET	/images/header_pic.jp.					
http://demo.testfire.n...	GET	/images/home1.jpg					
http://demo.testfire.n...	GET	/images/home2.jpg					

Figure 4-8. *List of requests*

The next section numbered as '3' as per Figure 4-6 is shown in
Figure 4-9. This section shows the actual HTTP request and response.
You can see the raw request by default but also see the request in form of
parameters. You can also see all of the headers used in the response.

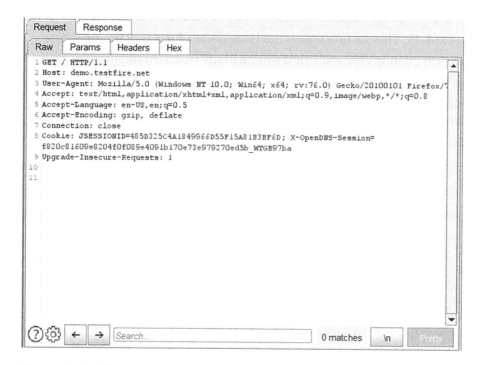

Figure 4-9. *The request and response viewer*

The next section numbered as '4' as per Figure 4-6 is shown in Figure 4-10. This section shows the list of issues that were found either during the passive scan or active scan. The issues are classified as per the severity, with highest severity issues being shown at the top.

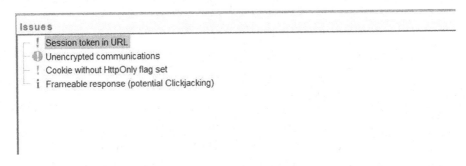

Figure 4-10. *Issues found in the target application*

The next section numbered as '5' as per Figure 4-6 is shown in Figure 4-11. This section shows the issue details for any of the selected issues. It contains the issue description along with remediation recommendations. In this section it is also possible to view the actual request and response based on which the issue was highlighted.

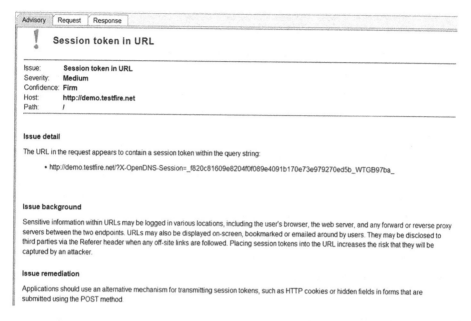

Figure 4-11. *Issue details*

The next section numbered as '6' as per Figure 4-6 is shown in Figure 4-12. Once we configure our browser to work along with the Burp Suite, a lot of traffic may get captured. Hence to filter out only the required data, several filters can be used. Some common and useful filters include filtering by request type, MIME type, status code, extension, etc. This feature also allows searching for a particular item within the data collected through proxy.

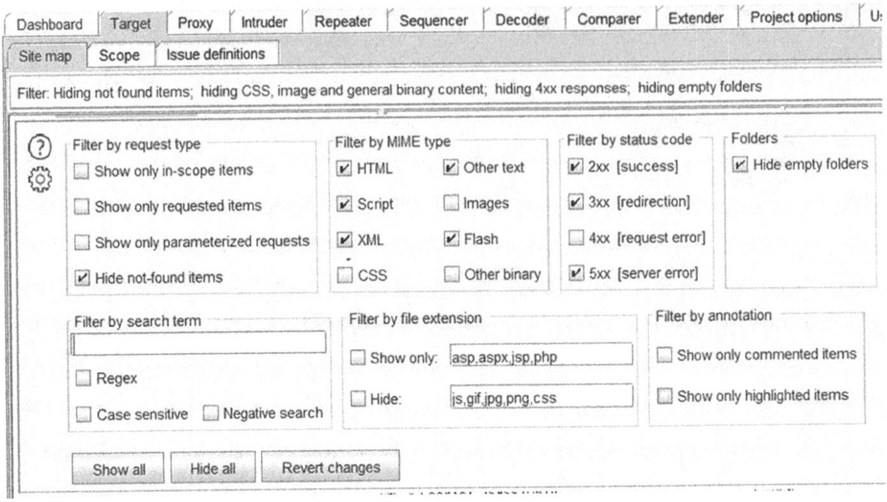

Figure 4-12. *Site map filters*

Engagement Tools

Engagement tools are nothing but small utilities that help in performing some additional tasks within Burp Suite. In this section we'll go through several such engagement tools serving different purposes. To access the engagement tools, simply right-click the target URL against which you wish to run the engagement tools as shown in Figure 4-13.

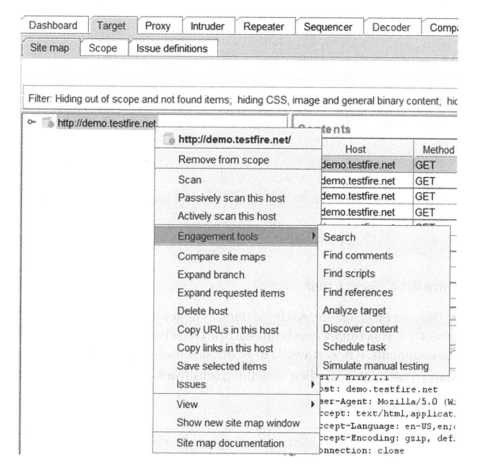

Figure 4-13. *The Burp Suite Engagement Tools*

The first engagement tool is the simple search as shown in Figure 4-14. This allows users to search for any keyword within the requests or responses from the target selected.

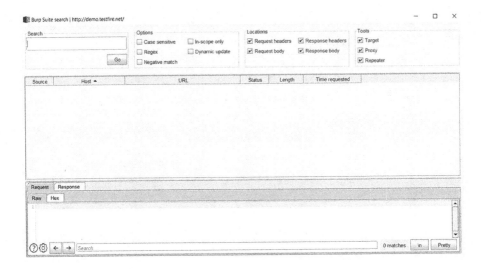

Figure 4-14. *Search tool*

The next engagement tool is the 'Find comments' as shown in Figure 4-15. This simply crawls through the collected data and finds any code comments. It is worthwhile to go through these comments as there's always a possibility of finding something sensitive in the comments.

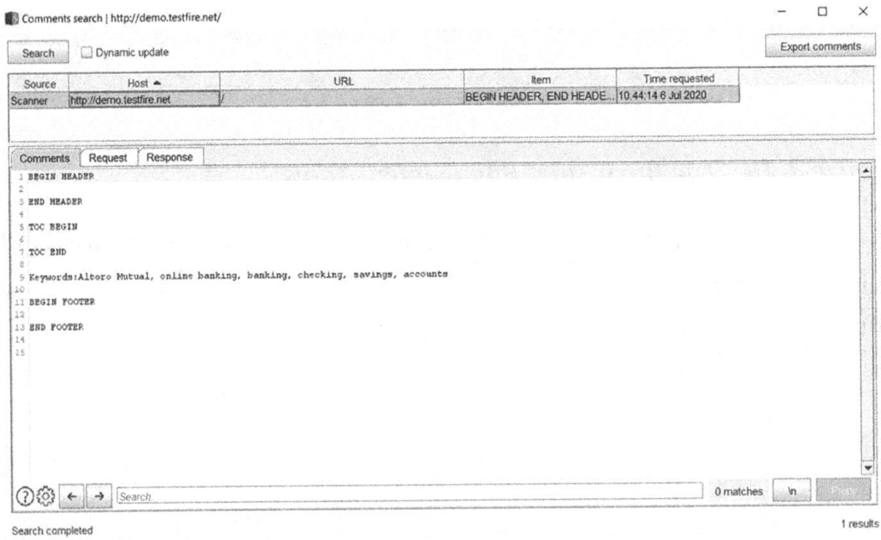

Figure 4-15. *Comment finder tool*

The next engagement tool is the 'Find scripts' as shown in Figure 4-16. This tool simply searches for all scripts within the scope of the target being selected.

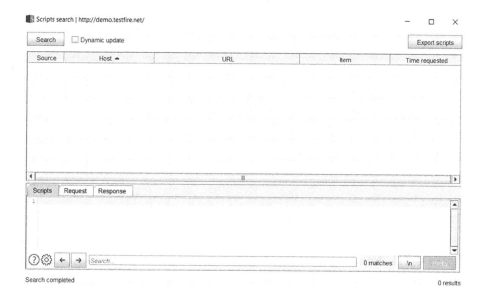

Figure 4-16. *Script searching tool*

The next engagement tool is the 'Find references' as shown in Figure 4-17. This tool lists down all the Burp Suite components where it is able to find any reference of the selected target. For example, the URL 'demo.testfire. net' appeared in Scanner as well as Target within the Burp Suite as shown in Figure 4-17.

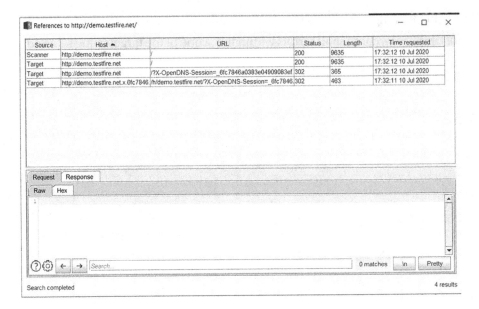

Figure 4-17. *Reference finder tool*

The next engagement tool is the 'Target Analyzer' as shown in Figure 4-18. This utility provides statistics mostly around sizing of the application in terms of the number of dynamic URLs, number of static URLs, number of parameters, etc. These statistics help the tester to get an estimate of effort that will be required to test the application.

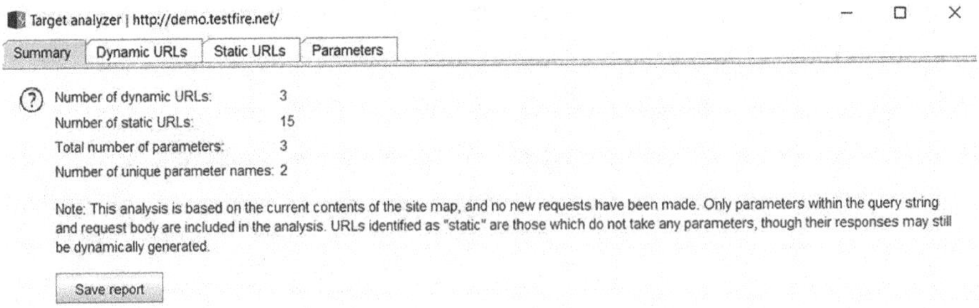

Figure 4-18. *The target analyzer*

The next engagement tool is the 'Content Discovery' as shown in Figure 4-19. This tool helps define the spidering or crawling rules. For instance, this helps define spidering rules when a new target is discovered, like how much length and breadth of it should be spidered or whether to spider only files or directories as well. This creates a well-structured sitemap. This is optional and can be left as the default.

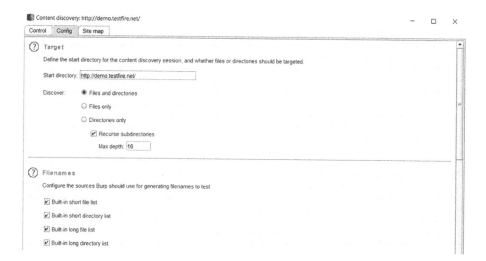

Figure 4-19. *The content discovery tool*

The next engagement tool is the 'Schedule Task' as shown in Figure 4-20. This is a simple utility to schedule any of the Burp Suite tasks. Using this you can either pause or resume any of the tasks.

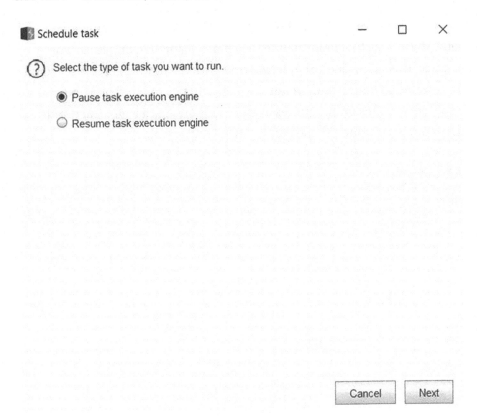

Figure 4-20. *The Burp Suite task scheduler*

The next engagement tool is the 'Manual Testing Simulator' as shown in Figure 4-21. This tool will send out HTTP requests to the target at random intervals and can help keep the session alive. This can be helpful in a scenario where the tester is on break and there's a possibility of the application session getting timed out due to inactivity.

Manual testing simulator   —   □   ✕

(?) This function sends common test payloads to random URLs and parameters at irregular intervals, to generate traffic similar to that caused by manual penetration testing. Its only real use is to let you take a break from testing while still looking busy according to the server's logs. Only items which you selected in the site map will be requested.

☐ Simulation running

Requests made: 0
Bytes transferred: 0
Errors: 0

Current Action

Host:
Path:
Parameter:
Base value:
Modified value:

Figure 4-21. *Manual testing simulator*

Summary

In this chapter we learned the basics of the Burp Suite dashboard, target tab, and also discussed several useful engagement tools.

In the next chapter we'll learn about how the Burp Suite Intruder can be used to automate attack scenarios like Brute Force, etc.

Exercises

- Browse through any of the target URLs of choice and observe the changes in the dashboard and target tab.

- Run each of the engagement tools against the selected target.

CHAPTER 5

Intruder

In the last chapter, we saw some basics about the Burp Suite dashboard, target, and engagement tools. Now that we have seen the basics of intercepting requests and interpreting the summary on the dashboard, we will move ahead with using the Intruder tool. Intruder has advanced fuzzing capabilities that can be used in various attack scenarios.

Introduction to Intruder

Before we get into the details of various options within Intruder, it's important to understand what Intruder is and how it can be helpful in web application security testing. Intruder is part of Burp Suite, which can be used effectively for fuzzing and performing a brute force attack.

There might be an application with a login page wherein the user needs to enter credentials to proceed further. From a security testing perspective, it would be worthwhile to test this login page for default credentials, weak passwords, or lockout mechanisms. This is where Intruder can come in handy. Given a list of usernames and passwords, Intruder can try all those combinations to see if any of them match.

We can also consider another scenario wherein we have an interesting request that we wish to investigate further to check if it's vulnerable to SQL injection or cross-site scripting. Again, Intruder can help with this. We can simply point Intruder to the URL and parameter we wish to test and feed

© Sagar Rahalkar 2021
S. Rahalkar, *A Complete Guide to Burp Suite*,
https://doi.org/10.1007/978-1-4842-6402-7_5

it with a list of SQL injection or cross- site scripting payloads. It will then try and insert all the payloads we provided into the parameter we want to test and get us the responses. Once this is done, we need to check the responses to see if any of the payload actually resulted in exploitation of the vulnerability.

Thus Intruder tremendously helps in any of the test scenarios where we have two of the following things:

1. A URL and a parameter to test

2. List of payloads to be submitted to the parameter

Now let's try to understand how we can send a request to Intruder. We have already seen the target tab and the hotkeys in previous chapters. Any request can be sent to Intruder in two ways:

1. Right-click the request you wish to send and click on 'Send to Intruder' as shown in Figure 5-1.

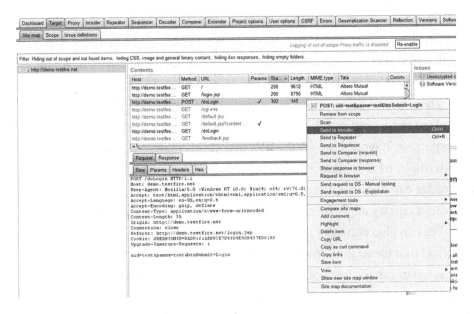

Figure 5-1. *Send request to Intruder*

2. Select the request you want to send and press the
    hotkey combination 'Ctrl + I'.

Now that we have sent the request to Intruder, let's see what options
need to be configured further.

Target Tab

The first tab in Intruder is the Target tab. This lists the target URL and port
that we wish to attack through Intruder as shown in Figure 5-2.

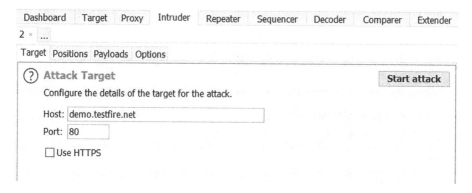

Figure 5-2. *Configuring the attack target in Intruder*

There's also an option to use HTTPS in case the target URL is using a
secure communication channel.

Positions

The next tab within Intruder is the Positions tab as shown in Figure 5-3.

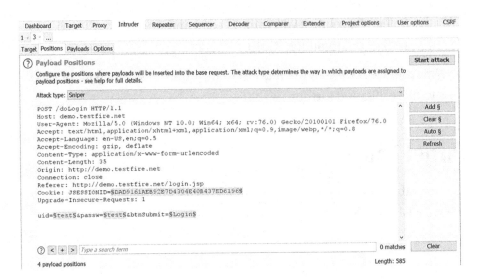

***Figure 5-3.** Configuring the positions in Intruder*

Whenever a request is sent to Intruder, it scans the request for probable insertion points and marks them as variables preceding and ending with the '$' sign. There are three options with regard to selecting the insertion points:

1. **Add $ –** This option is used to add a new insertion point. Simply point the cursor to the start and end of the insertion point and click on 'Add $'.

2. **Clear $ –** This option will simply remove all the insertion points that were either selected manually or automatically.

3. **Auto $ –** This option will scan the request and try to automatically set insertion points marking them with the '$' sign.

Once we are sure about the insertion points or parameters that we want to target, the next step is selecting the type of attack. There are four different attack types available as shown in Figure 5-4.

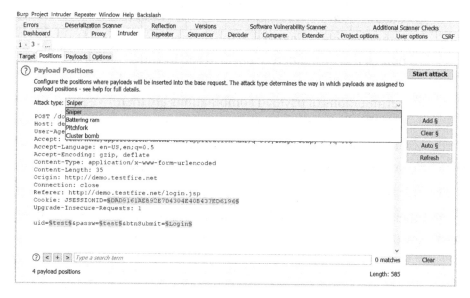

Figure 5-4. *Selecting the attack type in Intruder*

The four attack types are the following:

1. **Sniper –** This type of attack uses a single set of payloads. In this case Intruder inserts payloads into each of the insertion points at once and then iterates through it.

2. **Battering ram –** This type of attack uses a single set of payloads. In this case Intruder iterates through payloads by inserting the same payload at all insertion points at once.

3. **Pitchfork –** This type of attack uses multiple sets of payloads. In this case Intruder uses different payload for each of the insertion points.

4. **Cluster bomb** – This type of attack uses multiple sets of payloads. For each of the defined insertion points, there's a different payload set. Intruder iterates through each of the payload sets and all permutations of payload combinations are then tested. Due to the number of possible permutations and combinations in the case of a cluster bomb, a large number of requests would be generated.

Choosing the correct attack type depends on the attack scenario and the number of insertion points that need to be targeted simultaneously. See Figure 5-5.

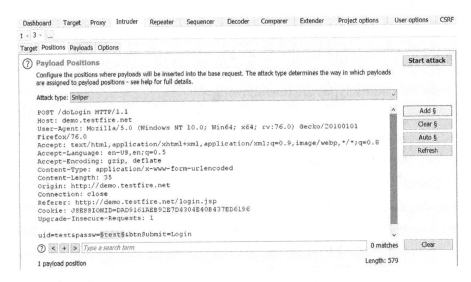

Figure 5-5. *Attack type and positions in Intruder*

Once the payload positions are configured and type of attack is selected, we can move ahead to configuring the actual payloads.

Payloads

Payload is the data that Intruder would iteratively insert in the selected insertion points. Payloads can differ widely based on the scenario or the attack that we are targeting. In the case of the login page that we are discussing, the payload would be a list of probable passwords. Burp Suite provides various payload types and the most commonly used one is the list. You can create your own list by adding elements one at a time as shown in Figure 5-6 or you can also select a predefined list that Burp Suite offers readily.

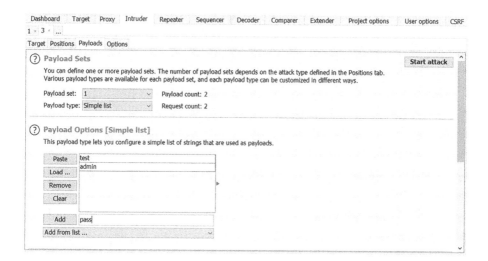

Figure 5-6. *Selecting payloads in Intruder*

Burp Suite has several predefined lists in the form of usernames, passwords, short words, fuzzing payloads for SQL injection and cross-site scripting, directories, extensions, etc. Depending on the type of attack, we can either use the predefined list or create our own list as shown in Figure 5-7.

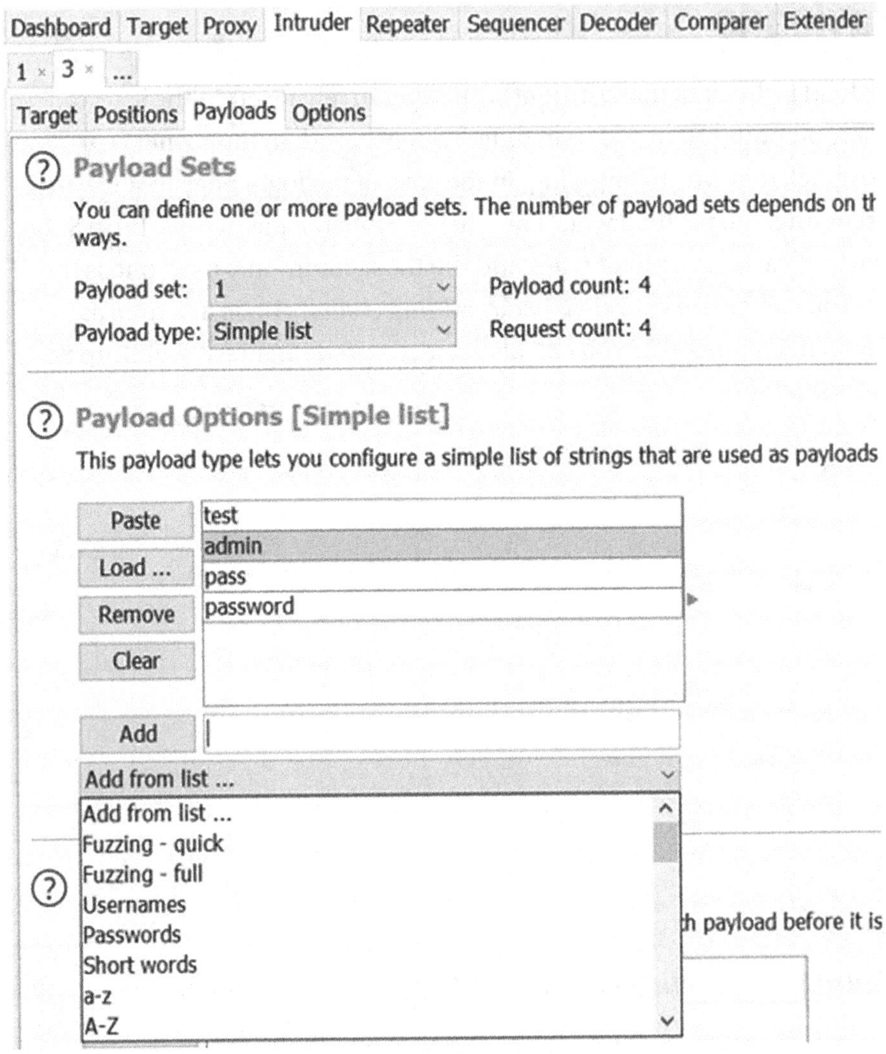

Dashboard Target Proxy Intruder Repeater Sequencer Decoder Comparer Extender

1 × 3 × ...

Target Positions Payloads Options

(?) **Payload Sets**

You can define one or more payload sets. The number of payload sets depends on th
ways.

Payload set: 1 ⌄   Payload count: 4

Payload type: Simple list ⌄   Request count: 4

(?) **Payload Options [Simple list]**

This payload type lets you configure a simple list of strings that are used as payloads

Paste	test
Load ...	admin
Remove	pass
Clear	password

| Add | | |

Add from list ...   ⌄

Add from list ...   ^
Fuzzing - quick
Fuzzing - full
(?) Usernames   th payload before it is
Passwords
Short words
a-z
A-Z   ⌄

Figure 5-7. Selecting Intruder payloads from various options

Now that we have configured the positions as well as the payloads, we
can launch the attack by clicking the 'Start attack' button. A new window
will pop up as shown in Figure 5-8, and the payloads we provided will be
submitted in insertion points we defined earlier – one request at a time.

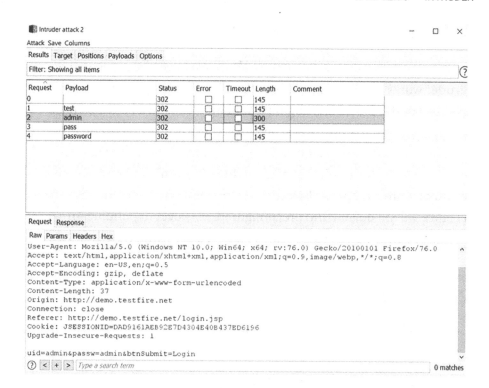

Figure 5-8. *Intruder attack results*

From Figure 5-8, we can see that Intruder sent five requests each with a different payload. Upon observing and comparing the content length, we can notice that for payload 'admin' the response was different. Hence it could be the password for the admin user we are trying to log in. We can then easily verify this by manually logging into the target application.

Options

The last part of Intruder is the 'Options' tab. We have already seen that Intruder works as a fuzzing tool or it can perform a brute force attack. This implies the Burp Suite engine would have to send a large number of requests, await the responses, and then process them based on a predefined ruleset. The 'Request Engine' option as shown in Figure 5-9 helps configure the number of parallel threads, number of retries on the network failure, and pause before the retry duration. The values as shown in Figure 5-9 are default and preconfigured. However depending on specific use cases, these values can be tailored accordingly.

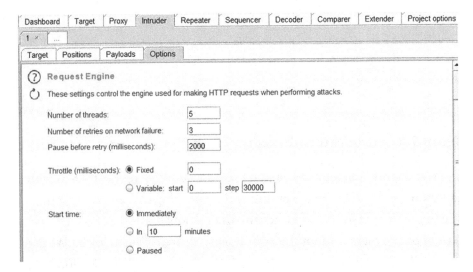

Figure 5-9. *Intruder configuration options*

Intruder sends a large number of requests to the target along with several permutations and combinations of payloads. The responses can be overwhelming to go through. This is where the 'Grep Match' feature comes in handy as shown in Figure 5-10. With this feature we can configure the Intruder engine to flag or highlight interesting responses having keywords like error, exception, illegal, fail, stack, access, directory, etc. If Intruder finds these keywords in any of the responses, they will be explicitly highlighted, making the analysis much easier.

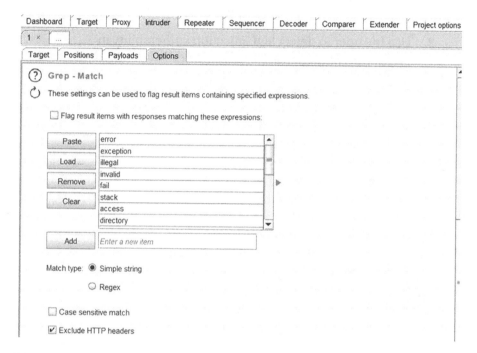

Figure 5-10. *Extracting relevant data from Intruder results*

Summary

In this chapter we learned about using the Intruder tool to perform fuzzing and brute force attacks. We started off the chapter by learning how to send requests to Intruder, configuring positions, payloads, and finally launching the attack and interpreting the results. We also saw some of the configurable options for Intruder.

In the next chapter we'll see some additional useful tools within the Burp Suite like Repeater, Comparer, Decoder, and Sequencer.

Exercises

1. Use Intruder to detect cross-site scripting vulnerability in any of the vulnerable applications.

2. Use Intruder to detect SQL injection vulnerability in any of the vulnerable applications.

CHAPTER 6

Repeater, Comparer, Decoder, and Sequencer

In the last chapter we learned about how Intruder can be used for fuzzing and performing brute force attacks. In this chapter we will look at some more Burp Suite tools like Repeater, Comparer, Decoder, and Sequencer.

Repeater

Repeater, as the name suggests, is a simple tool within Burp Suite that helps in replaying requests. We have already seen in previous chapters that when we browse an application through Burp Suite, a large number of requests are captured. Not all of the captured requests can be helpful for further testing or analysis. However, there could be a handful of requests with interesting parameters that are worth spending time on for further analysis. Repeater helps precisely in this scenario. If we find a particular request worth investigating further, we can simply send it to Repeater. Once in Repeater, we can play around with the request the way we want; tamper its headers, parameters etc.; and then send the request to the application and see how it responds. Repeater is a very simple yet powerful tool and has an easy interface as shown in Figure 6-1.

© Sagar Rahalkar 2021
S. Rahalkar, *A Complete Guide to Burp Suite*,
https://doi.org/10.1007/978-1-4842-6402-7_6

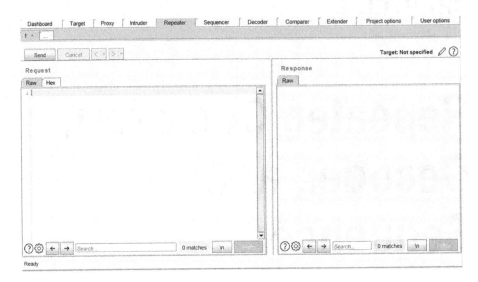

Figure 6-1. *The Repeater console*

The Repeater tab can be directly accessed in Burp Suite. By default it opens up empty and we need to feed it with an appropriate HTTP request data. To specify the target, click on the 'edit' icon next to 'Target' and a new window will pop up as shown in Figure 6-2, where we can enter Host and Port details we wish to interact with.

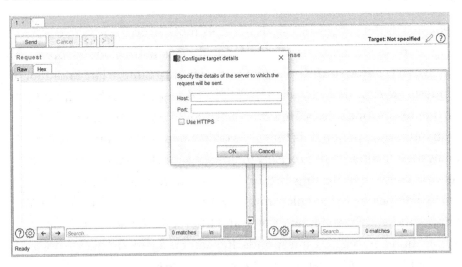

Figure 6-2. *Configuring the target details in Repeater*

The more convenient way of sending data to Repeater is as shown in Figure 6-3. Simply right-click any of the requests that you wish to send to Repeater for further analysis and click on 'Send to Repeater.' Another alternative is jto ust select the request to be sent to Repeater and press the hotkey 'Ctrl + R.'

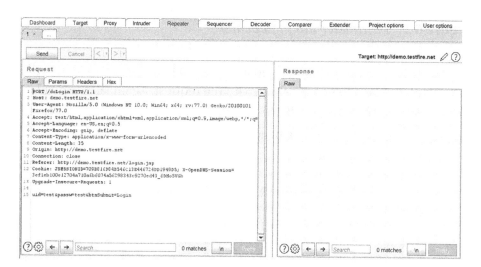

Figure 6-3. *Sending HTTP request to Repeater*

The request to be investigated is now sent to Repeater as shown in Figure 6-4. The request tab contains the HTTP request we selected and the response tab is blank as we haven't sent the request yet.

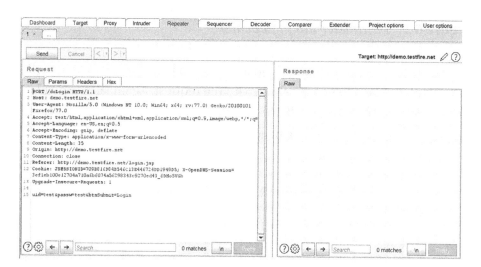

Figure 6-4. *Raw HTTP request in Repeater*

The Request window has several tabs within as shown in Figure 6-5. One of the tabs is 'Params', which lists all the parameters associated by default with the request we loaded. We can edit the existing parameters, add new parameters, or even delete any of the existing parameters. It is always interesting to see how the application responds to all of these parameter edits.

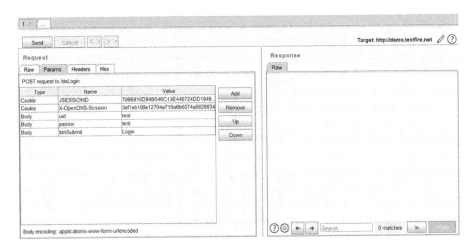

Figure 6-5. *Parameter tab in Repeater*

The next tab is the 'Headers' tab as shown in Figure 6-6, which lists all the default headers to be sent along with the request. Again, all the header values are editable: we can edit the existing values, add new header fields, and remove any of the existing header fields as well.

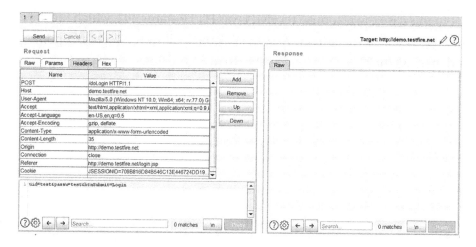

Figure 6-6. *Headers tab in Repeater*

Once we set the required parameters and header values, we can click on the 'Send' button as shown in Figure 6-7 and we get a response from the application, which is shown in the 'Response' tab.

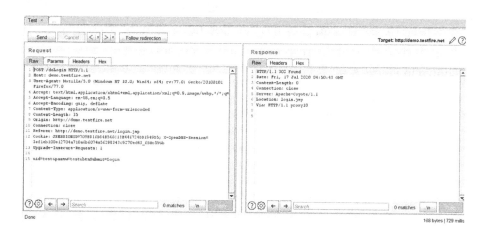

Figure 6-7. *Response tab in Repeater*

83

In this case the response received was HTTP status 302, which means the page is meant to redirect. We can click the 'Follow redirection' option and then get the final response as shown in Figure 6-8.

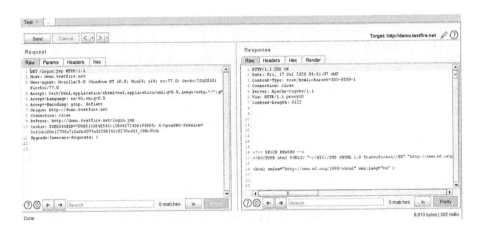

Figure 6-8. *Response tab in Repeater*

The response shown here is raw text and at times can be difficult to interpret. Hence we can click the 'Render' tab within the 'Response' section to visually load the response as if we were seeing it in the browser, as shown in Figure 6-9.

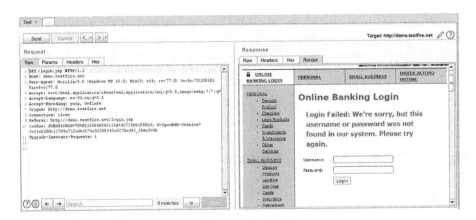

Figure 6-9. *Rendering the response in Repeater*

Repeater also provides an option to view the response in the real browser. To do this, simply right-click on the response that you wish to see in the browser, and click on 'Show response in browser' as shown in Figure 6-10.

Figure 6-10. *Viewing the response in the Browser*

Burp Suite will pop up another window as shown in Figure 6-11, with a link that needs to be copied into the browser.

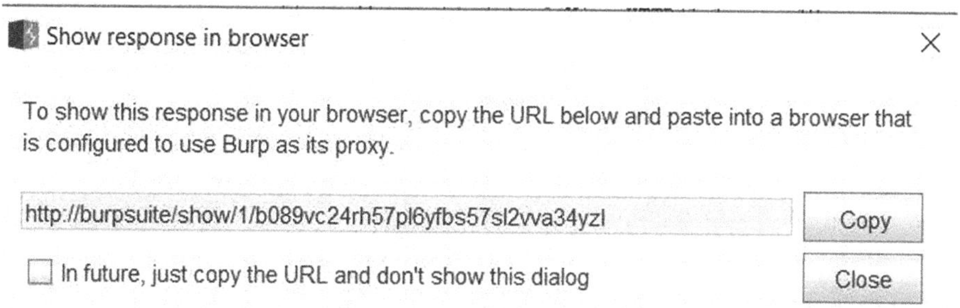

Show response in browser   ✕

To show this response in your browser, copy the URL below and paste into a browser that is configured to use Burp as its proxy.

http://burpsuite/show/1/b089vc24rh57pl6yfbs57sl2vva34yzl | Copy |

☐ In future, just copy the URL and don't show this dialog | Close |

Figure 6-11. *Show response in the Browser*

Once the link generated by Burp Suite is copied in the browser, the response gets rendered accordingly.

Comparer

In the last section we got familiar with the Repeater tool. Once the request is sent to Repeater, there is wide scope to tamper the request parameter or header fields and send it across to the target application. The responses in each case may vary depending on what parameters or header fields that were set in the request. There could be multiple responses, each of them looking quite similar. This is where the Comparer tool comes in handy. Comparer simply compares content head to head and highlights differences if there are any. To send a response to Comparer, simply right-click the response and click on 'Send to Comparer' as shown in Figure 6-12.

Figure 6-12. *Sending Repeater response to the Comparer*

Now as the Comparer needs at least two text blocks to compare, we send another response to Comparer as shown in Figure 6-13.

Figure 6-13. *Sending Repeater response to the Comparer*

We can now navigate to the Comparer tab as shown in Figure 6-14 and see both responses that we sent from Repeater earlier.

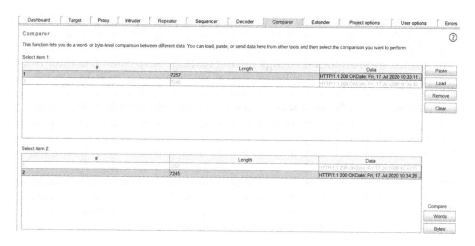

Figure 6-14. *The Comparer console*

Now since we need to find differences in words from both of the responses, we click on the 'Words' button and get a new window opened as shown in Figure 6-15.

Figure 6-15. *Comparing the responses in the Comparer*

Comparer will now highlight the text changes in two of the parallel windows.

Decoder

Web applications commonly use various encoding schemes like Ascii, HTML, Base 64, etc. From a security testing perspective, it's very common to encounter such encoded strings during testing. Burp Suite Decoder is a simple utility that can encode or decode text in a format of a URL, HTML, Base 64, ASCII hHx, Hex, Octal, Binary, and Gzip. Simply navigate to the Decoder tab as shown in Figure 6-16 and enter the text that needs to be decoded.

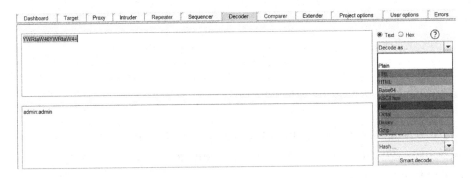

Figure 6-16. *Decoding Base 64 data*

In this case we entered a Base 64 encoded value and then clicked on 'Decode as' Base 64 to get the decoded output in the next window as admin:admin.

We can also use this tool to encode any plain text as shown in Figure 6-17.

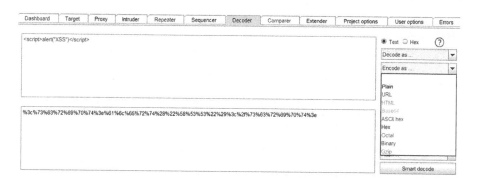

Figure 6-17. *Encoding data using the Burp Suite Decoder*

We simply entered the plain text <script>alert("XSS")</script> and then clicked on 'Encode as' the URL to get the encoded output in the next window.

Sequencer

Web applications depend a lot on tokens, session IDs, or other such unique and random identifiers. From a security perspective, it is important to test the randomness or uniqueness of these tokens and identifiers. If the tokens aren't strong and random enough, then attackers can easily brute force them and get unauthorized access.

Burp Suite Sequencer is a tool that helps us test the strength of application tokens. We can send any request to Sequencer just by right-clicking the request and clicking on 'Send to Sequencer' as shown in Figure 6-18.

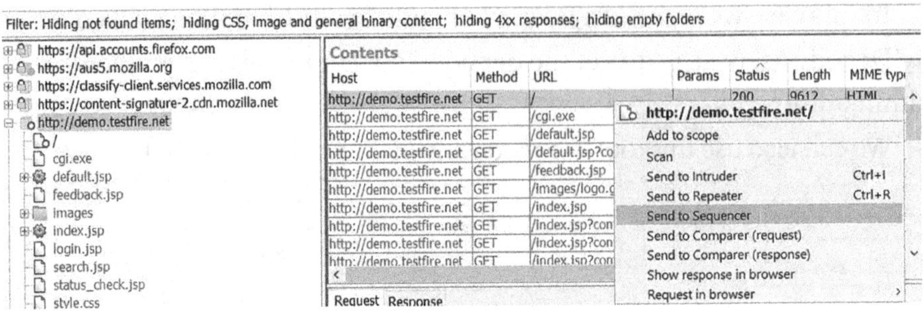

Figure 6-18. Sending HTTP request to Sequencer

We can now navigate to the Sequencer tab as shown in Figure 6-19.

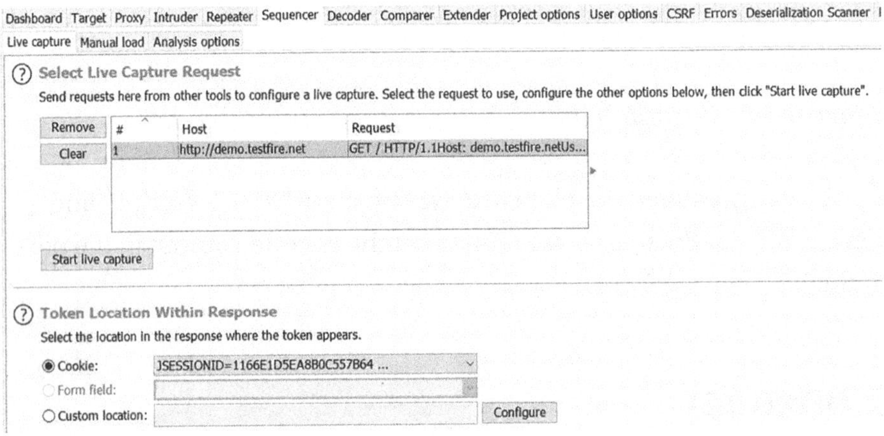

Figure 6-19. The Burp Suite Sequencer

We can clearly see the Sequencer has automatically parsed the request and selected the JSESSIONID token present in the cookie. This token would now be analyzed for its strength and randomness. To start the test, simply click on 'Start live capture' and a new window will open up as shown in Figure 6-20.

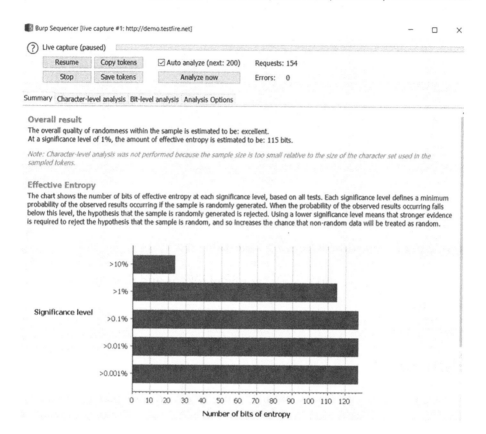

Figure 6-20. *Session ID analysis using Sequencer*

The live capture starts and we can pause or resume it any time we wish. However, it's important to note that to effectively analyze the token strength, a sample size of at least 100 should be considered. Once the capture is complete, Sequencer shows us the result, which was found to be "excellent" in this case. So the token JSESSIONID is strong, unique, random, and hence safe to use.

Sequencer also allows us to load a sample of tokens manually and then analyze them. To do this, simply navigate to the 'Manual load' tab in Sequencer as shown in Figure 6-21.

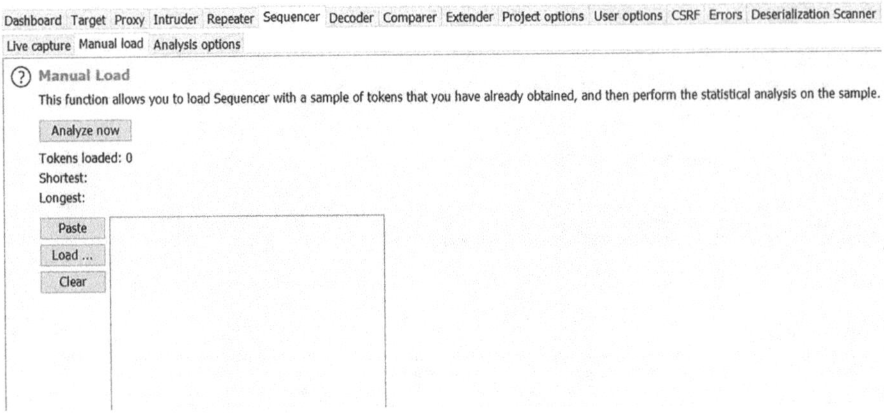

Figure 6-21. *Manually loading tokens for analysis*

We can now copy and paste a sample of tokens and then analyze them accordingly.

Summary

In this chapter we saw how to tamper and replay requests using Repeater, then perform a head-to-head comparison of responses using Comparer. We then learned about the Decoder tool, which helps encode and decode text in various formats. Lastly we got familiar with the Sequencer tool, which can be used to assess the effectiveness of tokens.

In the next chapter, we'll learn about some additional useful tools within the Burp Suite like Infiltrator, Collaborator, Clickbandit, and CSRF PoC Generator.

Exercises

1. Send any of the requests to Repeater and try to tamper with its parameters and header fields. Then send each of the requests and analyze the responses.

2. Compare the multiple responses using Comparer.

3. Use the Decoder tool to encode text in URL, HTML, and Base 64 formats.

4. Assess the token strength of the token from any of the requests captured.

CHAPTER 7

Infiltrator, Collaborator, Clickbandit, and CSRF PoC Generator

In the last chapter we looked at some Burp Suite tools like Repeater, Sequencer, Decoder, and Comparer. In this chapter we will continue to explore more useful tools like Infiltrator, Collaborator, Clickbandit, and CSRF PoC (proof-of-concept) generator.

Infiltrator

Burp Suite Infiltrator is a tool that instruments the target web application so that the vulnerability detection by the Burp Suite scanner becomes more efficient and accurate. Infiltrator makes irreversible changes in the code and essentially hooks into the target application. This way, it helps the Burp Suite scanner get more visibility into the application code and potentially detect unsafe calls and functions.

© Sagar Rahalkar 2021
S. Rahalkar, *A Complete Guide to Burp Suite*,
https://doi.org/10.1007/978-1-4842-6402-7_7

As the Infiltrator makes irreversible changes to the target application code, it is advisable to run it only for a test instance and not on a production instance. Currently, the Infiltrator is supported if the target application is using any of the following technologies:

- Java

- Groovy

- Scala

- Other JVM language (JRE versions 1.4 - 1.8)

- C#

- Visual Basic

- Other .Net language (.Net versions greater than 2.0)

To get started with the Infiltrator, click on the Burp menu and then select 'Burp Infiltrator' as shown in Figure 7-1.

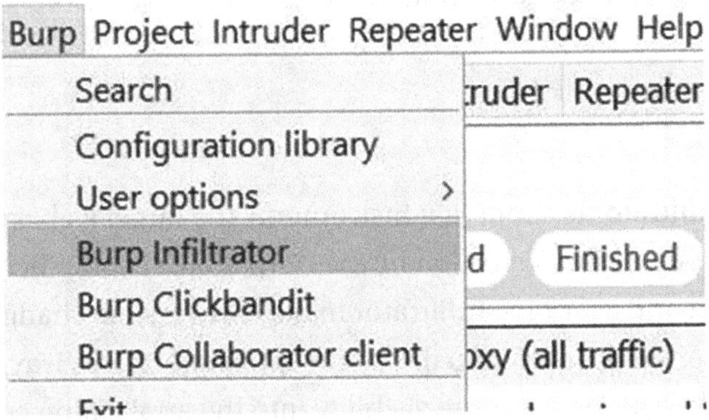

Figure 7-1. *Navigating to the Burp Suite Infiltrator*

A new window will pop up as shown in Figure 7-2. This wizard will help us generate the Infiltrator agent.

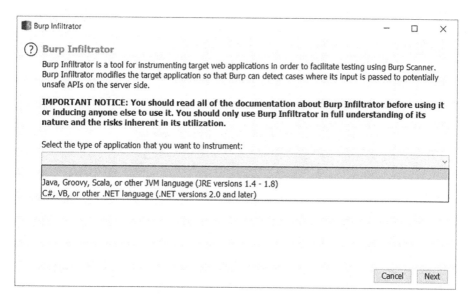

Figure 7-2. *Generating the Infiltrator agent*

We need to select the technology our application is using like Java or .NET and click on Next. Then the wizard will ask the location where we wish to save the Infiltrator agent, as shown in Figure 7-3.

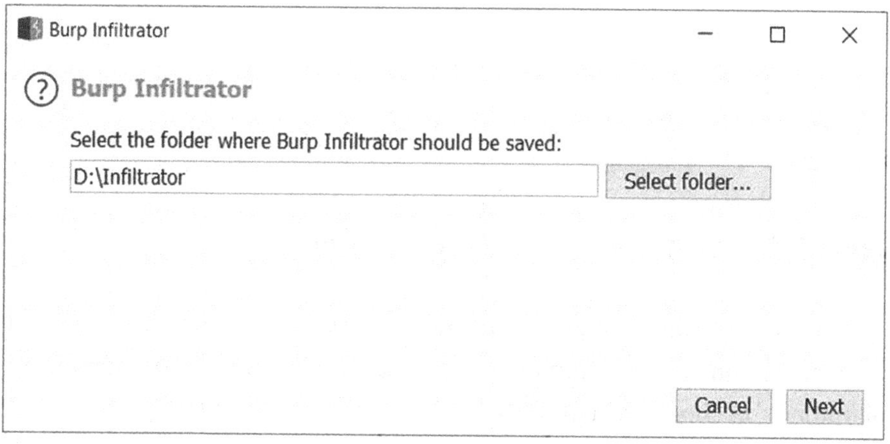

Figure 7-3. *Generating the Infiltrator agent*

Next, the wizard will simply generate the Infiltrator agent and save it to the location we selected earlier, as shown in Figure 7-4.

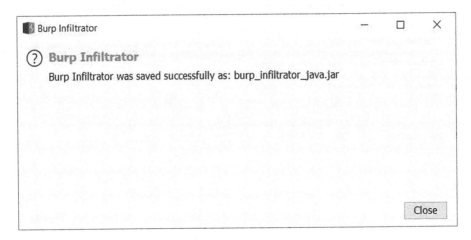

Figure 7-4. Generating the Infiltrator agent

The important thing to note here is the Infiltrator agent should be in the same directory where the target application is located as shown in Figure 7-5.

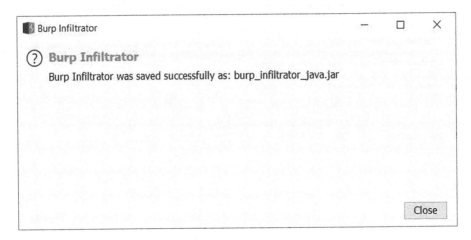

Figure 7-5. Newly generated Infiltrator agent

Now that both the Infiltrator agent and the target application are in the same directory, we can open a command prompt and type command 'java -jar burp_infiltrator.jar' as shown in Figure 7-6.

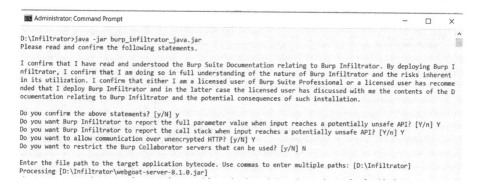

```
Administrator: Command Prompt                                        —    □    ×

D:\Infiltrator>java -jar burp_infiltrator_java.jar
Please read and confirm the following statements.

I confirm that I have read and understood the Burp Suite Documentation relating to Burp Infiltrator. By deploying Burp I
nfiltrator, I confirm that I am doing so in full understanding of the nature of Burp Infiltrator and the risks inherent
in its utilization. I confirm that either I am a licensed user of Burp Suite Professional or a licensed user has recomme
nded that I deploy Burp Infiltrator and in the latter case the licensed user has discussed with me the contents of the D
ocumentation relating to Burp Infiltrator and the potential consequences of such installation.

Do you confirm the above statements? [y/N] y
Do you want Burp Infiltrator to report the full parameter value when input reaches a potentially unsafe API? [Y/n] Y
Do you want Burp Infiltrator to report the call stack when input reaches a potentially unsafe API? [Y/n] Y
Do you want to allow communication over unencrypted HTTP? [y/N] Y
Do you want to restrict the Burp Collaborator servers that can be used? [y/N] N

Enter the file path to the target application bytecode. Use commas to enter multiple paths: [D:\Infiltrator]
Processing [D:\Infiltrator\webgoat-server-8.1.0.jar]
```

Figure 7-6. *Executing the Infiltrator agent*

The Infiltrator will now run and modify the Java applications in the directory. This is a one-time procedure, and the application needs to restart once the patched code is available. Burp Infiltrator also makes use of Collaborator, which we will be seeing in the next section.

Collaborator

Collaborator is a tool provided by Burp Suite that helps in attacks like Server Side Request Forgery (SSRF) or any of the out-of-band attacks. The Burp Suite Collaborator service helps by generating random payloads in the form of hostnames. These payloads can then be used as part of requests in various attack scenarios. If the attack is successful, then an interaction occurs between the target application server and the Burp Collaborator server. Then using the Burp Collaborator client, we can poll and check if any such interactions have happened.

To get started with the Burp Collaborator, simply click on the Burp menu and click "Burp Collaborator client." A new window will pop up as shown in Figure 7-7.

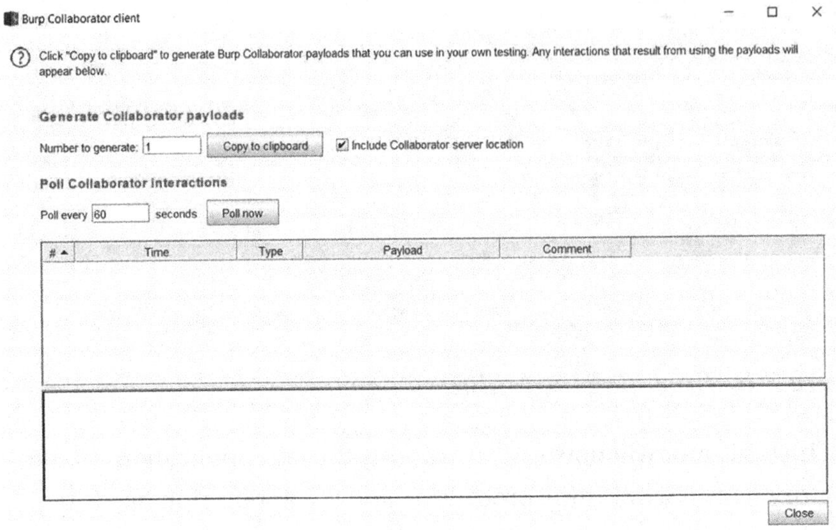

Figure 7-7. *The Burp Suite Collaborator client*

Now click on the 'Copy to clipboard' button and paste its value in the notepad as shown in Figure 7-8.

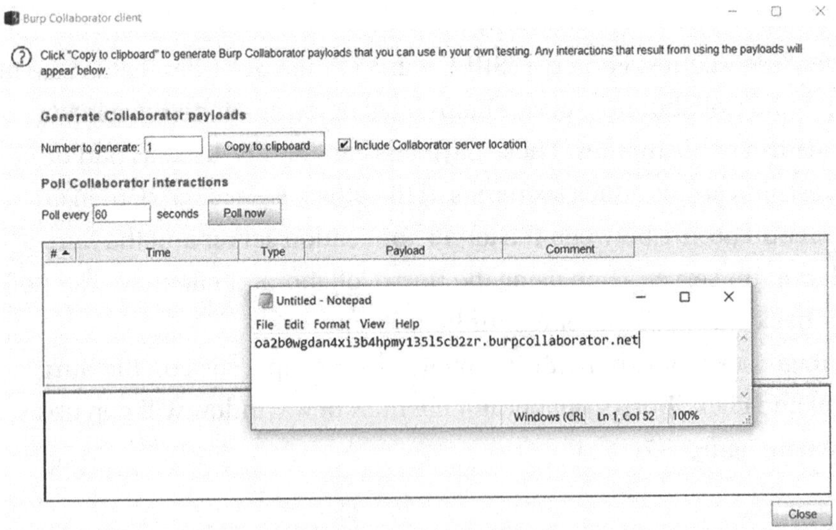

Figure 7-8. *Configuring the Collaborator client*

The random value generated by the Burp Collaborator can now be used in payloads in requests sent as part of an attack. The Burp Collaborator client automatically polls the Collaborator server after every 60 seconds to check if there has been any interaction. This duration can be customized or you can simply click on the 'Poll now' button to manually check for Collaborator interactions.

Clickbandit

Clickjacking is one of the very common attacks on web applications. Using clickjacking, the attacker tries to trick the user into clicking something different than what the user sees visually. If successful, the attacker can get access to confidential information. Clickjacking is also known as a UI redressal attack, as the attacker tries the deceptive technique of creating a fake UI and then tricks the victim into executing malicious actions or events.

Burp Suite offers a utility called 'Clickbandit' that significantly simplifies the process of generating Proof-of-Concept for an application that is vulnerable to Clickjacking.

To get started with the Clickbandit tool, simply go to the Burp menu and click on 'Burp Clickbandit'. A new window will pop up as shown in Figure 7-9.

Figure 7-9. *The Burp Suite Clickbandit tool*

This window has steps listed that we need to follow in order to generate the Clickjacking Proof-of-Concept. The first step is to click on the 'Copy Clickbandit to clipboard' button. The next step is to open the browser and press function key F12 to go into the browser console as shown in Figure 7-10.

Figure 7-10. *Target for Clickbandit*

To proceed further, we need to paste the Clickbandit code into this browser console, which we copied earlier as shown in Figure 7-11.

Figure 7-11. *Copying the Clickbandit code in browser console*

Once the code is copied into the browser console, simply press Enter and you'll notice the Burp Clickbandit UI appears on top of the page as shown in Figure 7-12.

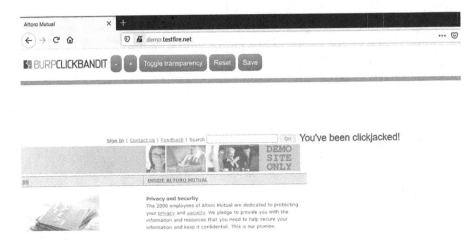

Figure 7-12. *The Clickbandit UI*

Now we need to perform and record the actions that we wish to include as part of the Clickjacking attack. Once all the required actions are done, click on the save button and you will be able to save a file named 'clickjacked.html' as shown in Figure 7-13.

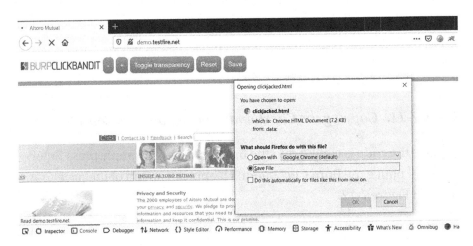

Figure 7-13. *Saving the Clickbandit code*

You can now open the file 'clickjacked.html' separately in the browser as shown in Figure 7-14.

Figure 7-14. *Executing the Clickbandit code*

You'll notice that the actions you captured earlier are now being replayed, and if you click, then you get a message 'You've been clickjacked!' as shown in Figure 7-15.

Figure 7-15. *Executing the Clickbandit code*

CSRF

Cross-Site Request Forgery, commonly known as CSRF, is another type of attack on web applications that exploits session management flaws to trick the victim into performing unwanted actions. Burp Suite has a utility that makes it very easy to generate Proof-of-Concept for CSRF vulnerability.

We first need to identify and confirm the request for which we wish to generate the CSRF Proof-of-Concept code. Once the request is finalized, simply right-click the request, go to 'Engagement tools', and click on 'Generate CSRF PoC' as shown in Figure 7-16.

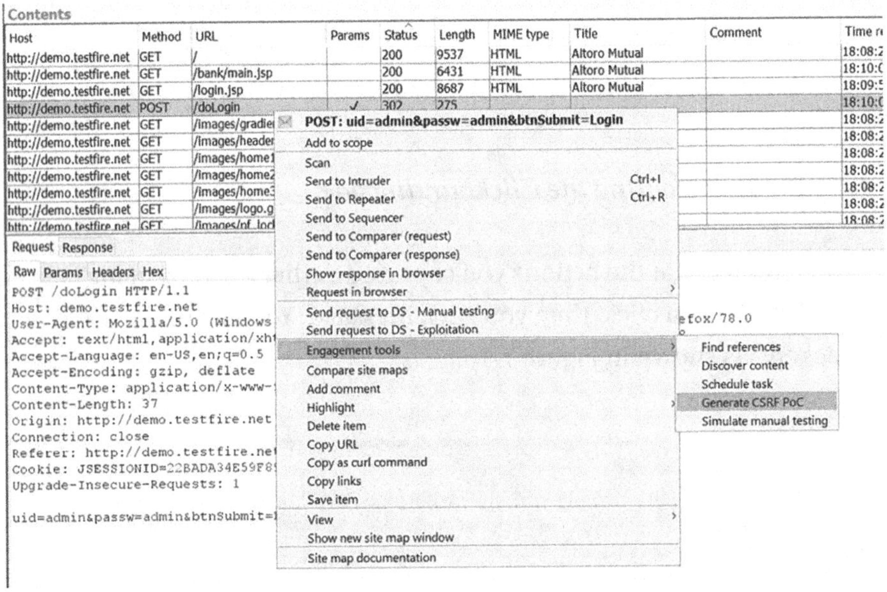

Figure 7-16. *Sending request to CSRF PoC generator*

Now, a new window will pop up as shown in Figure 7-17, which has the POST request along with the CSRF code.

Figure 7-17. *CSRF PoC generator*

It is now easy to modify the CSRF code as required and then we can either directly test it in the browser or generate a separate HTML file. To test the CSRF code in the browser, click on the 'Test in browser' button, and a new window will pop up as shown in Figure 7-18.

107

Figure 7-18. *CSRF PoC generator*

Now click on the 'Copy' button, open the browser, and paste into the address bar as shown in Figure 7-19.

Figure 7-19. *Verifying the CSRF PoC in browser*

Now click on the button 'Submit request', and the CSRF code will get executed as shown in Figure 7-20.

***Figure 7-20.** Verifying the CSRF PoC in browser*

Summary

In this chapter we learned about using Intruder for instrumenting applications and increasing detection capabilities of the Burp Scanner. Then we saw the Burp Collaborator, which can be effectively used in out-of-band attacks like SSRF. We then looked at the Clickbandit tool that helps generate proof-of-concept code for applications vulnerable to clickjacking; and lastly we glanced through the CSRF PoC generator, which helps us quickly generate and test proof-of-concept code for Cross-Site Request Forgery attacks.

In the next chapter, we'll see the automated scanning and reporting capabilities of the Burp Suite.

Exercises

1. Use Infiltrator to instrument any of your target Java applications.

2. Find a vulnerable CSRF request and try to generate a proof-of-concept using the CSRF PoC generator.

3. Generate a clickjacking proof-of-concept code for your target web application.

CHAPTER 8

Scanner and Reporting

In the last chapter, we learned about various tools like Infiltrator, Collaborator, Clickbandit, and CSRF PoC generator. In this chapter, we'll explore the features and capabilities of the Burp Suite scanner for automated vulnerability detection.

Scan Types

So far throughout the book, we have seen several capabilities of Burp Suite that are useful for manual testing. However, Burp Suite also provides a web application vulnerability scanner that automates the process of finding vulnerabilities. This is indeed a very feature-rich scanner and is capable of detecting potential web vulnerabilities.

The Burp Suite offers two types of scans: Passive Scan and Active Scan. The passive scan runs in the background, by default, while we browse an application through Burp Suite. A passive scan simply monitors the traffic and tries to list vulnerabilities like missing security flags in cookies, missing security headers, traffic being sent over unencrypted communication channels, etc. Thus the passive scanner doesn't attempt to inject any payloads into any of the insertion points, but rather just highlight vulnerabilities that can be found only by passively monitoring ongoing requests and responses. The active scan goes a step further and

© Sagar Rahalkar 2021
S. Rahalkar, *A Complete Guide to Burp Suite*,
https://doi.org/10.1007/978-1-4842-6402-7_8

tries to insert payloads into insertion points and check if parameters are vulnerable. Active scanning is a more intense technique; however, it does a better job in finding vulnerabilities that a passive scanner may never find. We'll now look further into the details of performing an active scan using Burp Suite.

Crawl and Audit

Active scanning is usually a two-step process. The first step involves crawling or spidering the application and the second step involves attacking the parameters with payloads. The Burp Suite scanner offers two options: either crawl and audit or just crawl. To start a new audit, go to the Dashboard tab and click on 'New scan' as shown in Figure 8-1.

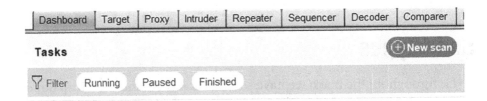

Figure 8-1. New scan task

A new window will pop up as shown in Figure 8-2. We select the option 'Crawl and audit'. Next, we need to specify the target URL that we wish to scan. In this case, we enter the target URL as 'demo.testfire.net'.

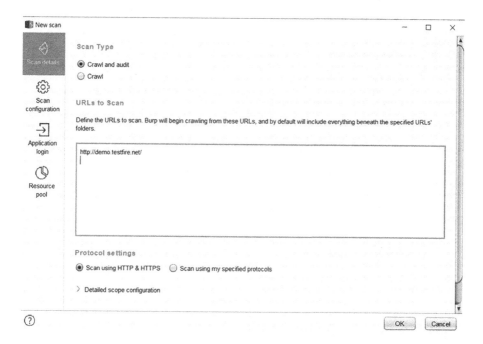

Figure 8-2. *New scan configuration*

Next is the scoping section as shown in Figure 8-3. The URL's that we wish to be part of the audit need to be specified under the 'Included URL prefixes' tab, and if there are any particular URLs that we don't want to be included in the audit, then those need to be explicitly added under 'Excluded URL prefixes.'

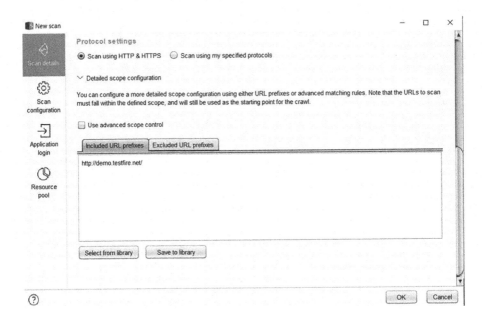

Figure 8-3. *New scan configuration*

Now that we have configured the target URL, we just need to click on 'OK' and the crawl and audit activity starts as shown in Figure 8-4. However, it's important to note that this activity will start with a default scan configuration.

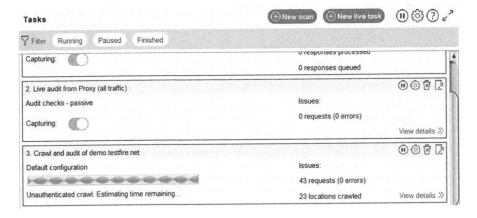

Figure 8-4. *Scan tasks in progress*

In the next section, we'll be looking at customizing the scan configuration.

Scan Configuration

In the previous section, we configured and initiated a crawl and audit task on a target URL but with default configuration settings. In this section, we'll take a look at how the scan configuration can be tailored to suit our needs. To customize the scan configuration, click on the 'Scan configuration' tab as shown in Figure 8-5.

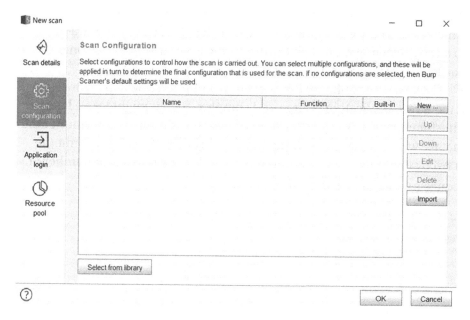

Figure 8-5. *Scan configuration*

The scan configuration allows us to customize crawl settings as well as the audit settings. We'll first go through the crawl configuration settings. Click on the 'New' button and select 'Crawl'. A new window will pop up as shown in Figure 8-6.

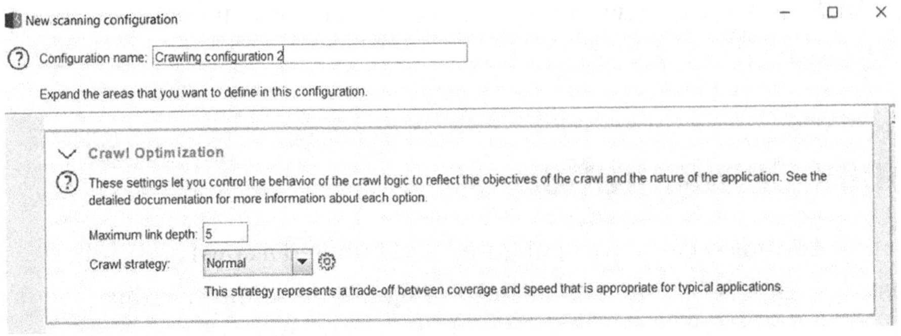

Figure 8-6. *Crawl optimization settings*

The crawl optimization configuration allows us to set the maximum link depth up to which we wish to crawl along with the crawl strategy, which is set to normal by default. We can change the crawling strategy to fast by selecting it through the drop-down menu, depending on the particular scan scenario.

Next, we can configure the crawl time limits as shown in Figure 8-7. If the target application is large and complex, then it might take a lot of time for crawling. We can set a limit to this by defining the maximum time that we wish to spend on crawling the application. We can also limit the crawl by the number of locations discovered or the maximum number of requests made during the crawl function.

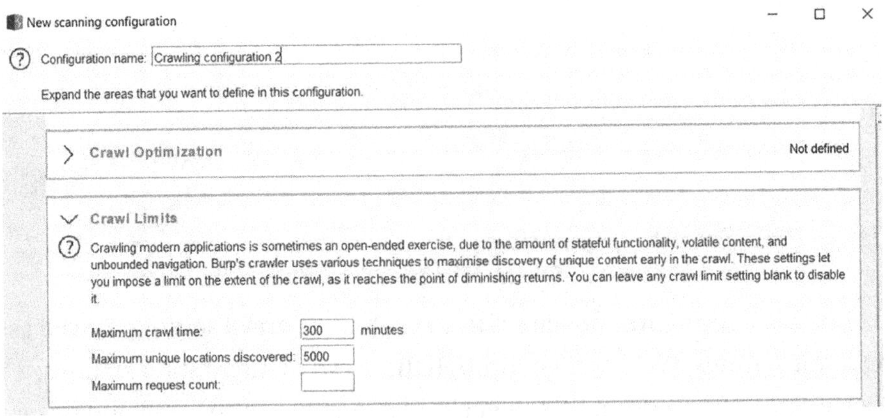

Figure 8-7. *Crawl limit configuration*

116

The next configuration setting is related to the login functions as shown in Figure 8-8. It might happen that the target application has a login function. In such a case, Burp Suite will even try to register a new test user.

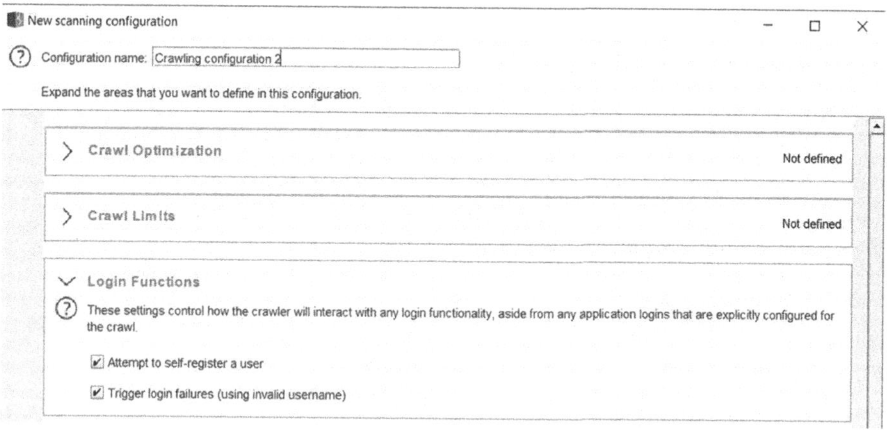

Figure 8-8. Login function configuration

The next configuration setting is related to handling application errors during a crawl function as shown in Figure 8-9. There could be multiple reasons behind application errors, like an authentication failure, network problems, etc. This configuration setting tells the Burp Suite scanner to pause the crawl and audit function if there are a certain number of consecutive application errors.

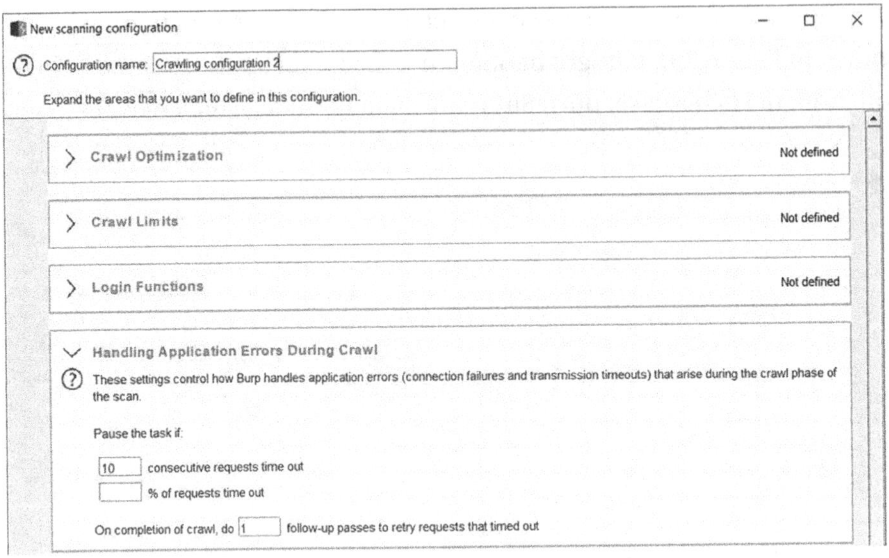

Figure 8-9. Configuring application errors during Crawl

The next set of configuration settings are miscellaneous as shown in Figure 8-10. This includes settings on whether we want the Burp Suite scanner to automatically submit forms or if we wish to customize the user-agent if we want to fetch robots.txt and the sitemap, etc.

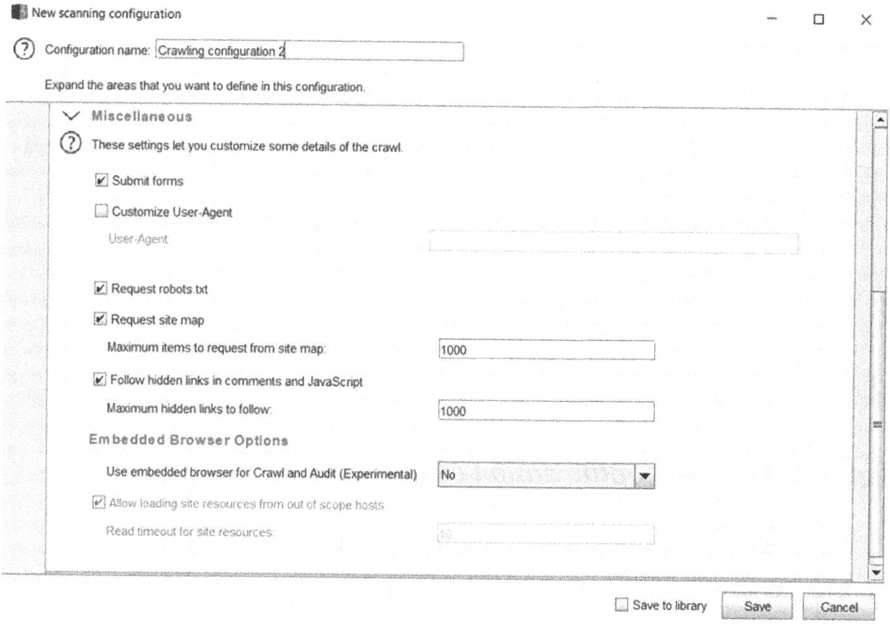

New scanning configuration   —   □   ×

(?) Configuration name: Crawling configuration 2

Expand the areas that you want to define in this configuration.

∨ Miscellaneous

(?) These settings let you customize some details of the crawl.

☑ Submit forms

☐ Customize User-Agent

User-Agent

☑ Request robots.txt

☑ Request site map

Maximum items to request from site map: 1000

☑ Follow hidden links in comments and JavaScript

Maximum hidden links to follow: 1000

Embedded Browser Options

Use embedded browser for Crawl and Audit (Experimental)   No   ▼

☑ Allow loading site resources from out of scope hosts

Read timeout for site resources:

☐ Save to library   Save   Cancel

Figure 8-10. Miscellaneous crawl configuration

The next set of configuration settings are related to the audit function. To start with, the first audit configuration setting is 'Audit Optimization' as shown in Figure 8-11. This setting allows us to configure audit speed and accuracy. The audit speed can be set to either fast, normal, or thorough, while the audit accuracy can be set to normal or to minimize false positives.

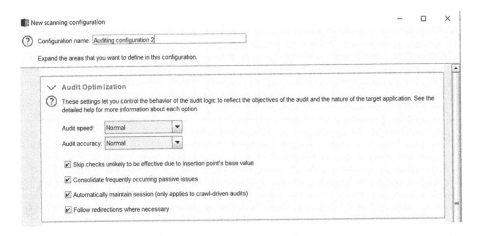

Figure 8-11. *Audit optimization configuration*

The next audit configuration setting is related to the type of issues reported as shown in Figure 8-12. The Burp Suite scanner detects a variety of issues. However, during a particular test scenario, it might so happen that only a particular type of issue needs to be tested. In such a case, it won't be worth spending time on testing all other types of issues. Hence this configuration setting allows us to customize the type of issues that we want to be tested during the scan.

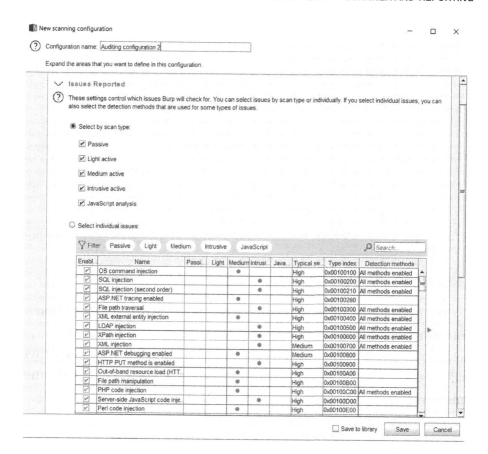

Figure 8-12. *Type of issues to be detected during an audit*

The next audit configuration setting is related to handling application errors during the audit function, as shown in Figure 8-13. We have already seen a similar configuration setting for the crawl function. This setting helps configure the number of failures after which the audit task would be paused.

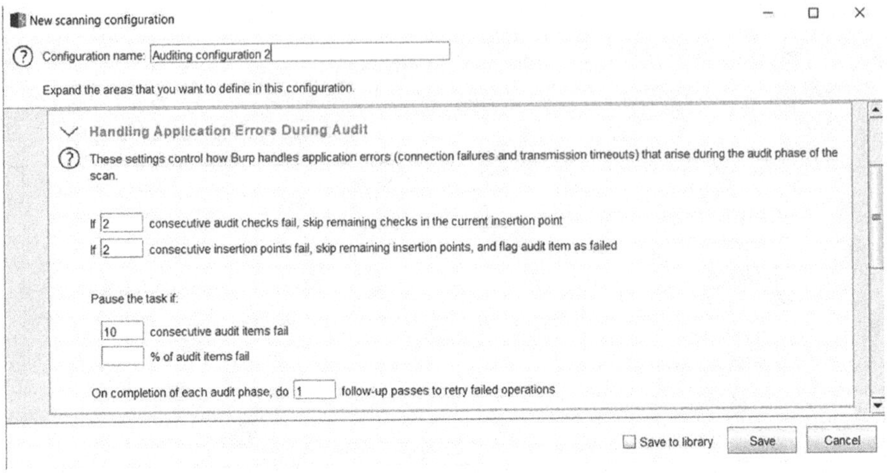

Figure 8-13. *Configuring application errors during Audit*

The next audit configuration setting is related to the type of insertion points that we want the Burp Suite scanner to attack during the audit function as shown in Figure 8-14. Selecting all the types of insertion points will increase the possibility of finding more vulnerabilities, but at the same time it will also take longer to finish the audit.

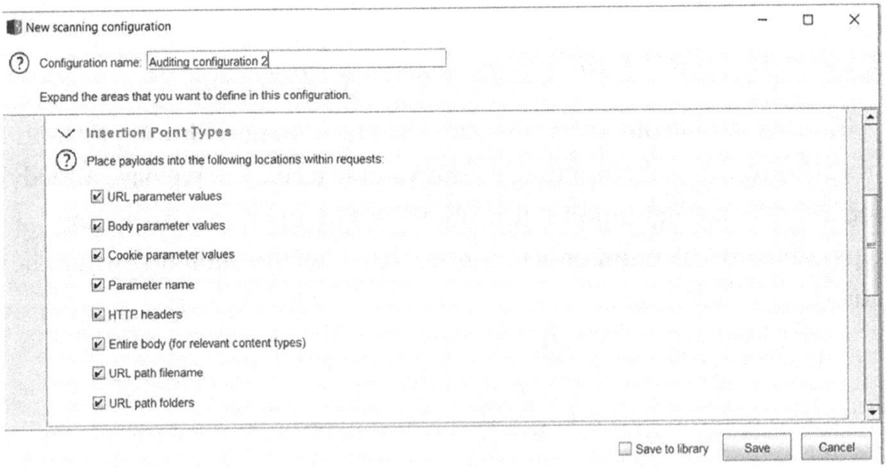

Figure 8-14. *Configuring insertion point types*

122

All the crawl and audit scan configuration settings we saw so far are set to optimal values by default. We can quickly trigger a new crawl and audit task using the default scan configuration. However, depending on particular scan scenarios, it might be required for you to customize the scan configuration settings.

Application Login

The next important scan configuration setting is configuring the 'Application login' as shown in Figure 8-15. While scanning the target application, we may come across certain pages that do not require authentication, while there could be a few pages that can be accessed only after authentication. If we want the Burp Suite scanner to audit the pages behind authentication as well, then we need to provide credentials.

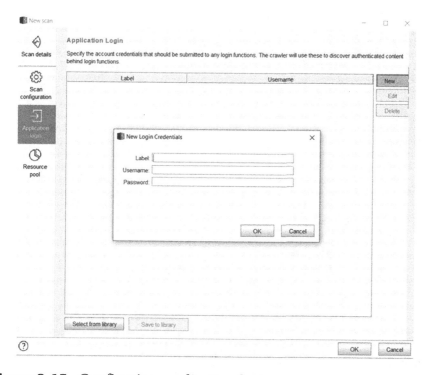

Figure 8-15. *Configuring application login*

123

Credentials can be added by simply clicking on the 'New' button and providing the required username and password.

Resource Pools

The last scan configuration option is "Resource Pool" as shown in Figure 8-16. The resource pool helps define the system resources that will be used across multiple tasks. By default, the resource pool is created, which allows for a maximum of 10 concurrent requests. We can leave this to default unless we want to do multitasking within the same Burp Suite project.

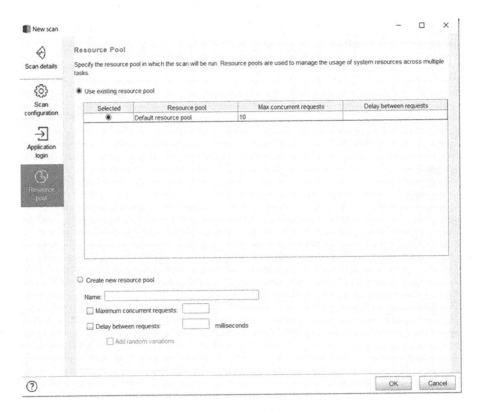

Figure 8-16. *Configuring resource pools*

Reporting

Reporting the issues in a presentable format is as important as finding them. Burp Suite offers an excellent reporting feature that helps us generate a report in the required format with all relevant extract about the vulnerability. The report, once generated, can be shared with relevant stakeholders for further action.

Once the crawl and audit task is complete, all the issues that were found during the scan are listed in the 'Issue activity' pane as shown in Figure 8-17. We now simply need to select the issues that we wish to be part of the report. To do this, simply right-click the issue that needs to be reported and click 'Report issue.'

Figure 8-17. *Exporting issues to report*

The Burp Suite reporting wizard will now ask us about the format of the report we wish to have as shown in Figure 8-18. Currently, the Burp Suite supports generating reports in HTML or XML formats.

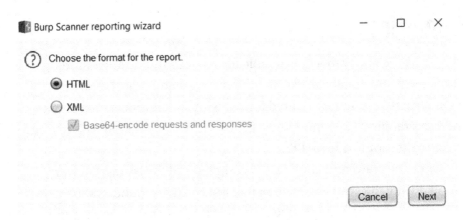

Figure 8-18. *Selecting format for the report*

Next, we need to select which details about the issue are required in the report as shown in Figure 8-19.

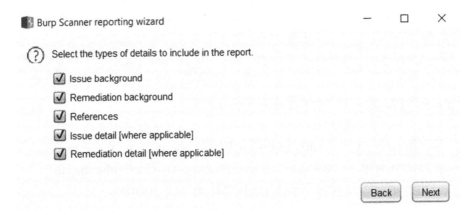

Figure 8-19. *Selecting type of details to be included in the report*

W then need to select whether we want full HTTP requests and responses for the reported issues or only the relevant extracts as shown in Figure 8-20.

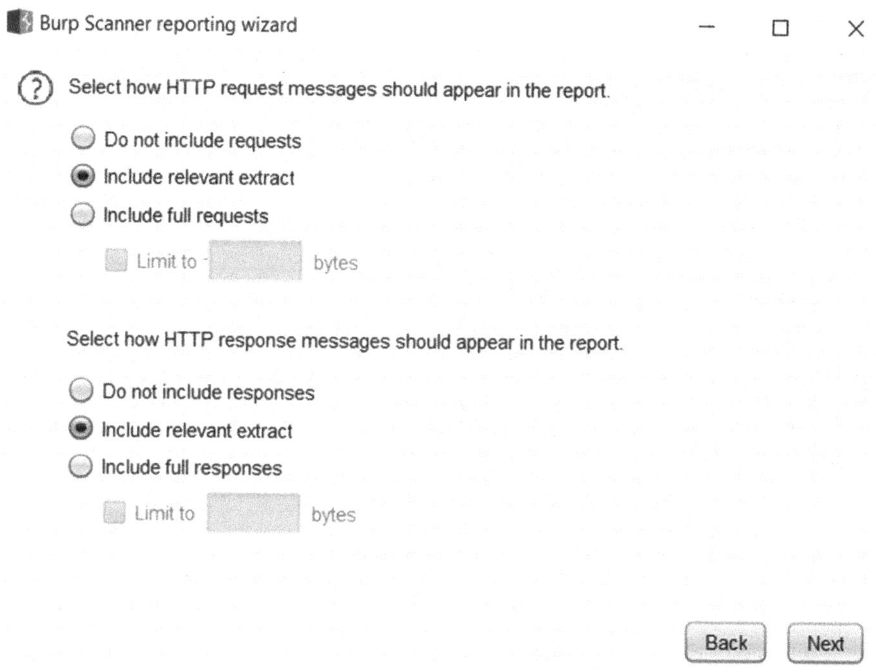

Figure 8-20. Selecting requests and response formats for report

Lastly, we need to select the name and location where we want the report to be generated along with the title of the report as shown in Figure 8-21.

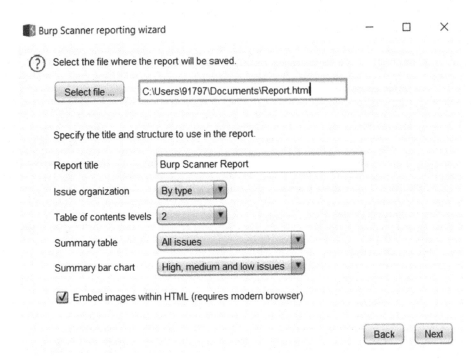

Figure 8-21. Configuring location where the report will be saved

Now the Burp Suite reporting wizard will generate a vulnerability report as shown in Figure 8-22.

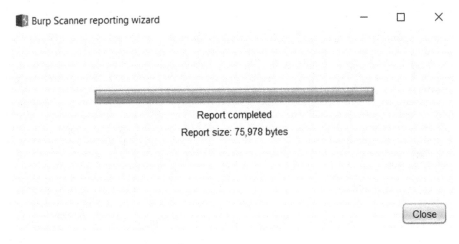

Figure 8-22. Generating the report

The generated report can them be viewed in any of the browsers as shown in Figure 8-23. The report shows a summary of findings based on confidence as well as severity.

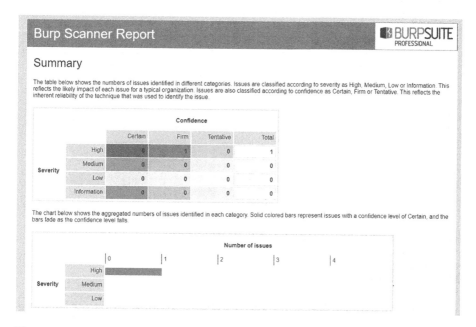

Figure 8-23. *Viewing the report in the browser*

The report also shows vulnerability in detail along with the relevant request and response as shown in Figure 8-24.

- CVE-2012-5568 - 5.0 - CVE-2012-5568
Apache Tomcat through 7.0.x allows remote attackers to cause a denial of service (daemon outage) via partial HTTP requests, as demonstrated by Slowloris.

Remediation detail

Issue background

Remediation background

Request

```
GET /index.jsp?content=business.htm HTTP/1.1
Host: demo.testfire.net
Accept-Encoding: gzip, deflate
Accept: /
Accept-Language: en-US,en-GB;q=0.9,en;q=0.8
User-Agent: Mozilla/5.0 (Windows NT 10.0; Win64; x64) AppleWebKit/537.36 (KHTML, like Gecko) Chrome/84.0.4147.89 Safari/537.36
Connection: close
Cache-Control: max-age=0
Referer: https://demo.testfire.net/robots.txt
Cookie: JSESSIONID=17F7DF68B17FA1C6865304C5138A0960
```

Response

```
HTTP/1.1 200 OK
Server: Apache-Coyote/1.1
Content-Type: text/html;charset=ISO-8859-1
Date: Sat, 08 Aug 2020 05:19:12 GMT
Connection: close
Content-Length: 8486

<!-- BEGIN HEADER -->
<!DOCTYPE html PUBLIC "-//W3C//DTD XHTML 1.0 Transitional//EN" "http://www.w3.org/TR/xhtml1/DTD/xhtml1-transitional.dtd">

<html xmlns="http://www.
...[SNIP]...
```

Figure 8-24. *Vulnerability details in the report*

Summary

In this chapter, we learned about the Burp Suite scanner and how it can be customized to effectively find application vulnerabilities in an automated manner.

In the next chapter we'll see how to use the Burp Suite Extender to install additional plugins and enhance the capabilities.

Exercises

1. Scan any of the target web applications using the crawl and audit function of Burp Suite.

2. Generate an HTML report for the issues found during the scan.

CHAPTER 9

Extending Burp Suite

In the last chapter, we learned about the Burp Suite scanner, which effectively helps in automating vulnerability detection. In this chapter, we'll be exploring the Burp Suite extender feature through which we can further enhance the capabilities of Burp Suite.

Burp Suite Extensions

So far, throughout the book, we have seen various capabilities of Burp Suite for manual as well as automated vulnerability detection. We have explored various tools and utilities within Burp Suite that can be leveraged for specific tasks.

Burp Suite has now evolved more like a platform that is flexible enough to accommodate external functionalities and utilities. As we have already seen, Burp Suite does provide numerous capabilities out of the box. However, these capabilities can be extended further using extensions.

The Burp Suite Extensions come in various forms as below:

Default extensions – These extensions are listed by default, out of the box in any of the Burp Suite setups, and can be installed through the Burp Suite Extender.

Pro extensions – These are extensions that can be installed and run only on the Burp Suite Professional Edition.

© Sagar Rahalkar 2021
S. Rahalkar, *A Complete Guide to Burp Suite*,
https://doi.org/10.1007/978-1-4842-6402-7_9

Regular extensions – These are extensions that can be installed and run on the Burp Suite Community Edition as well as the Professional Edition.

Other extensions – Burp Suite has opened up APIs that developers can write with new custom extensions. Such extensions are not part of the official extension store but need to be downloaded and installed manually.

BApp Store

The easiest way to install an extension in Burp Suite is through the BApp Store. To access the BApp Store, simply navigate to Extender ➤ BApp Store as shown in Figure 9-1.

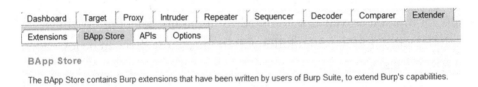

Figure 9-1. BApp Store

The BApp Store has a very easy-to-use interface with two panes as shown in Figure 9-2.

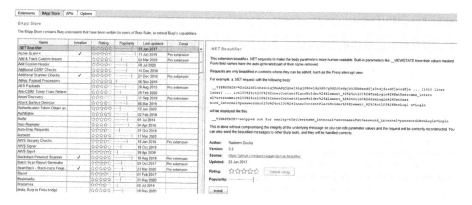

Figure 9-2. *BApp Store*

The left pane lists all the available extensions along with the following information:

- Name of the extension,

- Whether it is currently installed or not,

- Rating of the extension,

- The popularity of the extension,

- Date when the extension was last updated,

- Whether the extension is only available for use with the Burp Suite Professional Edition or if it can be used in the Community Edition as well.

The right pane details out information for any of the extensions we select from the left pane. This includes information like the following:

- Details on what the extension is about and how it can be used

- Author

- Extension version

- Source

- Date when the extension was last updated

- Rating and popularity of the extension

- Install button to install and add the extension to current Burp Suite setup

It is important to note that new extensions keep on getting added to the BApp Store on a regular basis. To ensure the list of extensions is the latest one, simply click on the 'Refresh list' button as shown in Figure 9-3.

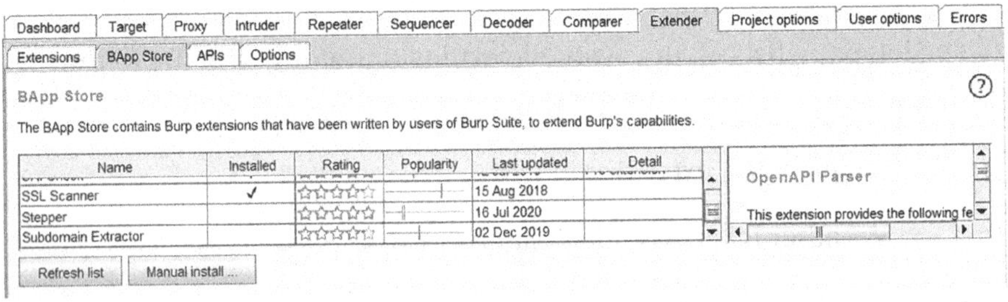

Figure 9-3. *Browsing through extensions in BApp Store*

Some of the useful extensions from the BApp Store are as follows:

- **Active Scan++ –** This extension is developed to further enhance the Burp Suite's passive and active scanning capabilities.

- **Additional Scanner Checks –** This extension adds a few more checks to a passive scanner like DOM-based XSS etc.

- **CSRF Scanner –** This extension helps passively scan for Cross-Site Request Forgery (CSRF) vulnerabilities.

- **Discover Reverse Tabnabbing –** This extension searches the HTML code for possible Tabnabbing vulnerabilities.

- **Error Message Checks –** This extension helps passively detect any error or exception messages that may contain sensitive information like stack traces.

- **Headers Analyzer –** This extension passively checks the response headers and flags all missing security headers like X-XSS-Protection, X-Frame-Options, and many more.

- **HTML5 Auditor –** This extension checks if any of the potentially unsafe HTML5 functions have been used like storing sensitive data on client-side storage, client geolocation, etc.

- **J2EEScan –** This extension helps improve test coverage for J2EE applications as well as adds additional test cases.

- **Java Deserialization Scanner –** This extension adds to the Burp Suite ability to detect Java Deserialization vulnerabilities.

- **JavaScript Security –** This extension further adds several passive checks related to JavaScript security like DOM issues, Cross-Origin Resource Sharing (CORS), etc.

- **Retire.js –** This extension passively monitors the traffic and detects the use of any vulnerable third-party library along with necessary CVE details.

- **SameSite Reporter –** This extension checks if the SameSite attribute has been set in cookies or not.

- **Software Version Reporter** – This extension passively parses the traffic and reports all the software version details. This information can further help in application enumeration.

- **Upload Scanner** – This extension adds capabilities to Burp Suite to detect file upload functionality and related vulnerabilities.

- **Web Cache Deception Scanner** – This extension scans the application for the presence of any Web Cache Deception vulnerability.

- **CSP Auditor** – This extension scans the response headers and checks if Content Security Policy (CSP) has been configured correctly or not.

- **CVSS Calculator** – This extension facilitates scoring vulnerabilities using CVSS methodology from within Burp Suite.

Manual Installation

In the previous section, we saw how we could browse through, select, and install extensions using the BApp Store. Not all extensions that are written are available in the BApp Store. There could be extensions written by individual authors, published on different websites like GitHub, etc. In such a scenario where the extension is not present in the BApp Store, we need to download it separately and install it manually. To install extensions manually, navigate to the 'Extensions' tab within Extender as shown in Figure 9-4.

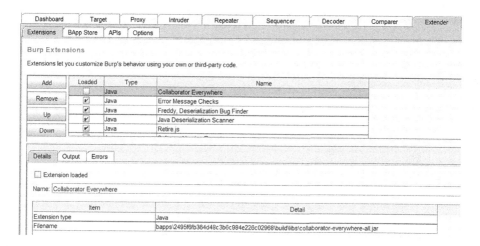

Figure 9-4. *Adding extensions manually*

Burp Suite accepts the installation of third-party extensions with the following formats as shown in Figure 9-5.

- Java

- Python

- Ruby

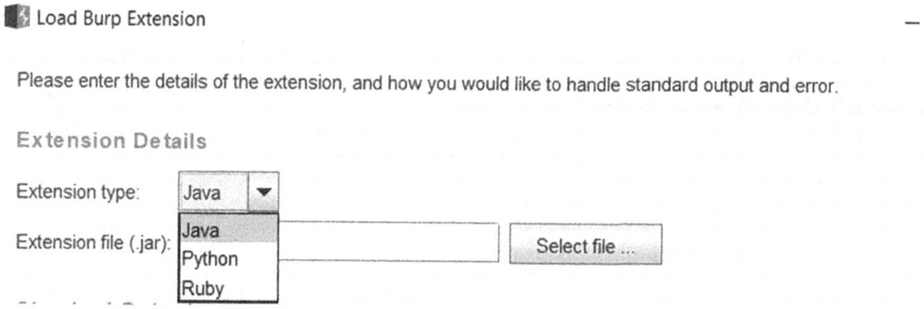

Load Burp Extension —

Please enter the details of the extension, and how you would like to handle standard output and error.

Extension Details

Extension type: Java ▼

Extension file (.jar):   Java / Python / Ruby   [Select file ...]

Figure 9-5. *Selecting type of the extension*

The other options include whether we wish to show the output and errors after extension installation on the console or if we wish to save it to a file as shown in Figure 9-6.

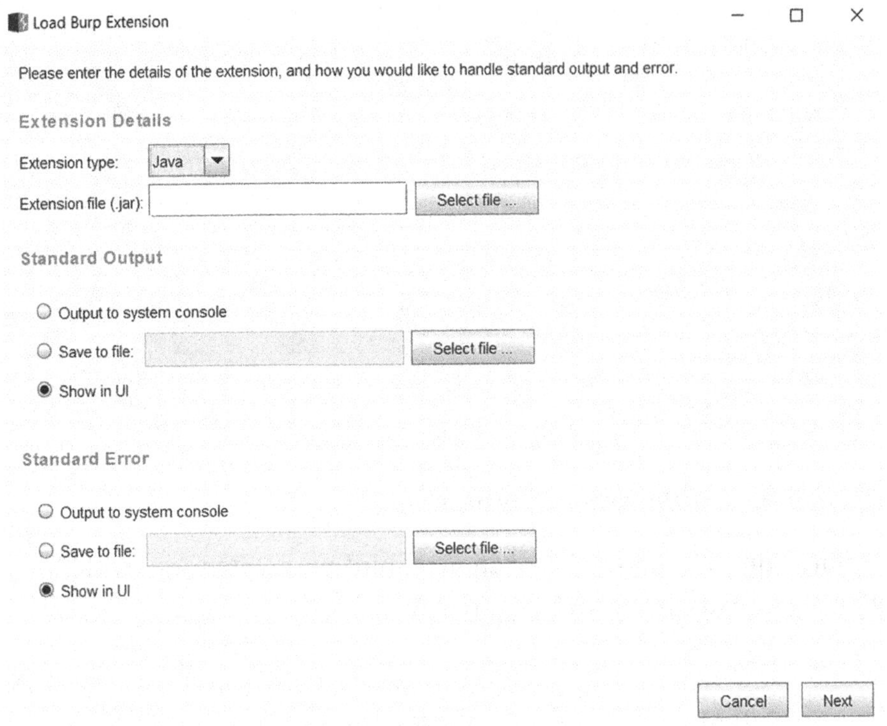

Figure 9-6. *Adding extensions manually*

To install an extension, select the extension type (Java / Python / Ruby) and then simply browse and select the location where the extension is located on disk as shown in Figure 9-7.

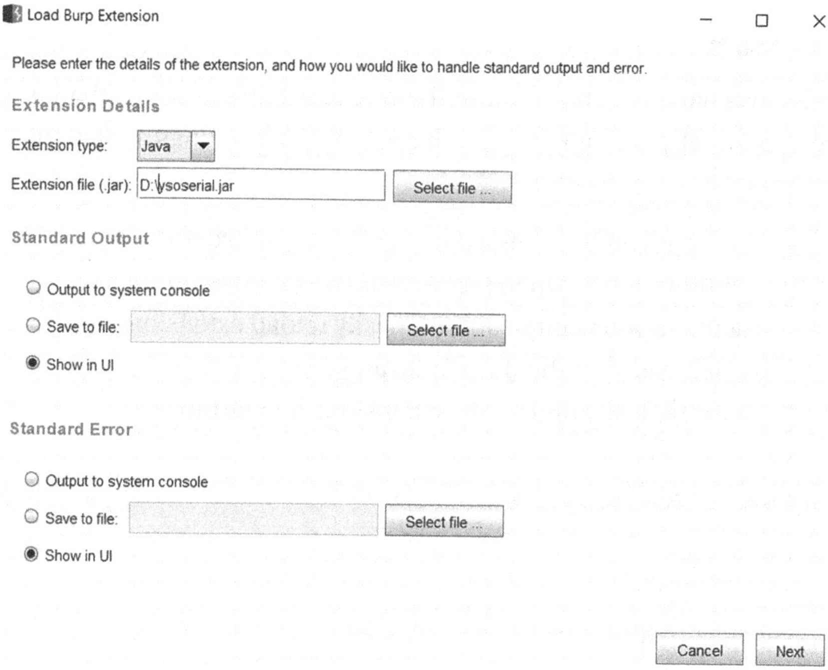

Figure 9-7. Selecting the extension file

If the extension installation gets completed successfully, a message is displayed as shown in Figure 9-8.

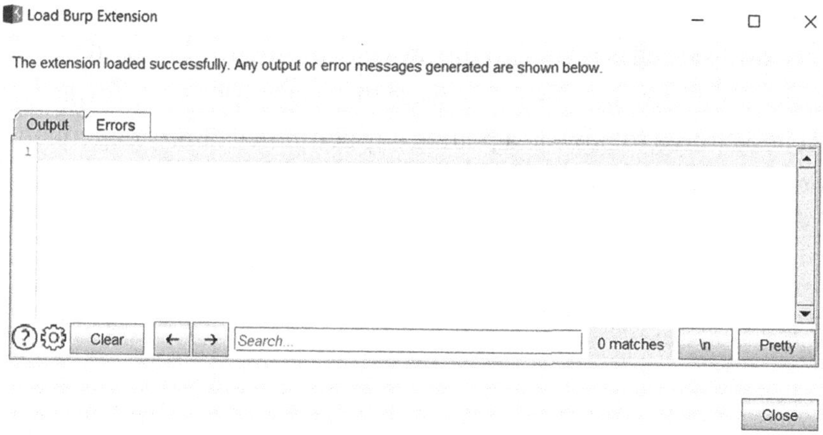

Figure 9-8. Loading extensions manually

Settings

Now that we have seen how to install extensions either through the BApp Store or manually, let's go through some additional settings related to extensions.

- Settings can be accessed by navigating to 'Extender ➤ Options' as shown in Figure 9-9. The first two settings define if you want to automatically reload extensions when you start the Burp Suite and if you wish to automatically update the extensions on Startup.

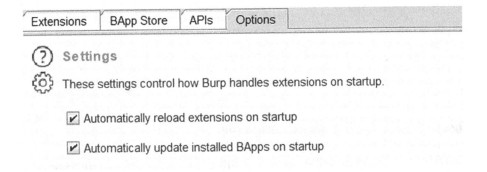

Figure 9-9. BApp Store options

The next setting is related to the Java environment. Most of the extensions are written in Java. To ensure these extensions run correctly, it might be required to provide a path to any additional library dependencies as shown in Figure 9-10.

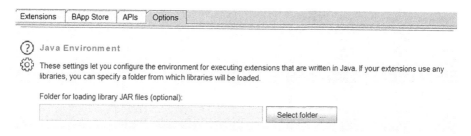

Figure 9-10. *Configuring the Java environment*

The next setting is related to setting up the Python environment. Some extensions require a Python interpreter implemented in Java called Jython. Jython can be downloaded and installed from `https://www.jython.org/download`. Once installed, you need to update the path to the Jython installation directory as shown in Figure 9-11.

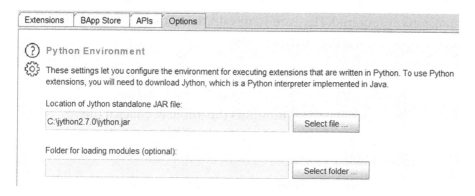

Figure 9-11. *Configuring the Python environment*

The last setting is related to setting up the Ruby environment. As we have seen earlier, Burp Suite supports extensions written in Ruby as well; hence we need to specify the path to the Ruby interpreter as shown in Figure 9-12. In order to run a Burp Suite extension written in Ruby, JRuby needs to be downloaded and installed from `https://www.jruby.org/download`.

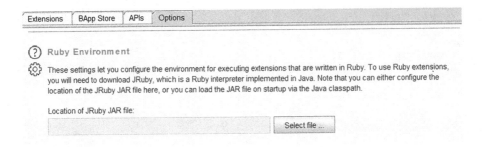

Figure 9-12. *Configuring the Ruby environment*

Other Useful Extensions

Earlier in this chapter, we already saw some useful extensions available in the BApp Store. As the Burp Suite gives Application Programming Interface (APIs) to developers, it is easy to write and develop custom extensions as required. Here are some additional useful extensions that can be manually installed to Burp Suite.

- **sometime** – This extension can be downloaded from https://github.com/linkedin/sometime. This extension passively monitors the traffic to check if the application is vulnerable to the Same Origin Method Execution.

- **burp-suite-gwt-scan** – This extension can be downloaded from https://github.com/augustd/burp-suite-gwt-scan - This extension helps automatically identify insertion points for GWT (Google Web Toolkit) requests when sending them to the active Scanner or Burp Intruder.

- **Admin panel finder** – This extension can be downloaded from https://github.com/moeinfatehi/Admin-Panel_Finder -This extension assists in the enumeration of infrastructure and application Admin Interfaces that might have been left open by mistake.

- **Pwnback** – This extension can be downloaded from `https://github.com/P3GLEG/PwnBack`. This extension helps to retrieve old and archived versions of the application if present. It can be useful to compare the old and current versions of the application to check the changes and associated vulnerabilities.

- **Minesweeper** – This extension can be downloaded from `https://github.com/codingo/Minesweeper` -This extension helps detect scripts being loaded from over 23000+ malicious cryptocurrency mining domains (cryptojacking).

For an additional and comprehensive list of the Burp Suite extensions, refer to `https://github.com/snoopysecurity/awesome-burp-extensions`.

APIs

Throughout this chapter, we have seen the use of Extender to add and install new extensions that significantly improve the Burp Suite capabilities. Burp Suite offers another useful feature in the form of the Application Programming Interface (API). Using these APIs it is possible to write our own extensions. The list of available APIs and detailed guidance on their usage is available under the 'Extender ➤ APIs' tab as shown in Figure 9-13.

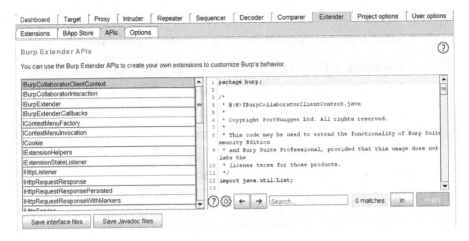

Figure 9-13. *The Burp Suite Extender APIs*

Summary

In this chapter, we got familiar with the Burp Suite extender, which allows enhancing the Burp Suite capabilities through external extensions. We explored the BApp Store, which has a list of many useful extensions and we also learned to install an extension manually in case it's not present in the BApp Store. Last, we listed a few additional extensions apart from those officially present in the BApp Store.

In the next chapter we'll see how we can leverage the Burp Suite capabilities to test mobile applications and APIs. We'll also see the complete workflow for testing an application using the Burp Suite.

Exercises

1. Use the BApp Store to install extensions discussed in this chapter.

2. Perform an active scan on the target application before installing the extensions and after installing the extensions. Observe the difference in vulnerabilities found in both the scans.

3. Explore the additional extensions discussed in this chapter and try to install them manually.

CHAPTER 10

Testing Mobile Apps and APIs with Burp Suite

In the last chapter, we learned about the Burp Suite extender feature, which allows enhancing the Burp Suite's capabilities through third-party extensions. In this final chapter, we'll glance through how Burp Suite can be used to test APIs and mobile applications as well. We'll conclude with a quick summary of the workflow for testing any web application using Burp Suite.

API Security Testing with Burp Suite

Throughout this book, we have been learning about various capabilities of Burp Suite, which can be used for Web Application security testing. However, today's modern applications are more interoperable and interconnected. This is achieved through the use of Application Programming Interfaces (APIs).

© Sagar Rahalkar 2021
S. Rahalkar, *A Complete Guide to Burp Suite*,
https://doi.org/10.1007/978-1-4842-6402-7_10

Exposing APIs significantly helps in automating tasks; however, at the same time, it does introduce security risks as well if not implemented securely. While most of the web application vulnerabilities apply to APIs, there are a few vulnerabilities that are specific to APIs. OWASP has published the Top 10 vulnerability list for API, which can be found at `https://owasp.org/www-project-api-security/`.

The approach for security testing of APIs through Burp Suite is very similar to the regular web applications that we have seen so far in the book. As APIs communicate over HTTP/HTTPS protocol, the traffic can be intercepted and tampered in Burp Suite just like any other regular web application request and response. For performing security testing on APIs using Burp Suite, we can use one of the following approaches:

1. Crawl the application in a regular way and figure out the endpoints belonging to APIs. Once the API endpoints are identified, the corresponding requests can be sent to the Repeater or Intruder for further testing.

2. Many times, the APIs are invoked through the User-Interface (UI) functionalities in the application. In such a case, you can simply create a new 'Crawl and Audit' task in the Burp Suite scanner and ensure all scanner checks and tasks are complete.

3. There could be a set of APIs that are not directly invoked from any of the UIs. Such APIs are often tested manually using tools like Postman. We can easily integrate Postman with Burp Suite to capture all required API traffic. Once the required API requests and responses are in Burp Suite, it is just a matter of testing them further using Repeater or Intruder as necessary.

We'll now see how we can integrate Postman with Burp Suite. Postman is a popular tool used for manual API testing. It can be downloaded from `https://www.postman.com/downloads/`. The Postman application interface is as shown in Figure 10-1.

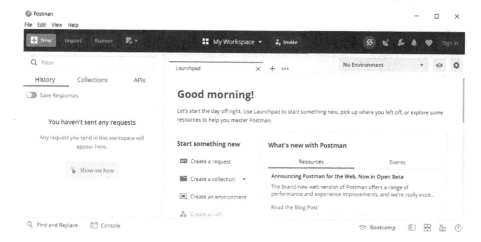

Figure 10-1. *The Postman tool*

In order to configure Postman to work along with Burp Suite, click on the 'Settings' option in the upper right corner as shown in Figure 10-2.

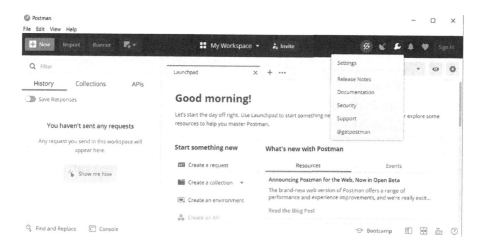

Figure 10-2. *Navigating to the settings in the Postman tool*

A new Settings window will open up as shown in Figure 10-3. Now further navigate to the proxy tab and select 'Add a custom proxy configuration' and enter the proxy server address as that of the machine running the Burp Suite (usually localhost or 127.0.0.1) and port as 8080 or the one on which we want the Burp Suite proxy listener to be active on.

SETTINGS

General   Themes   Shortcuts   Data   Add-ons   Certificates   Proxy   Update   About

☑ Use the system proxy

  ☐ Respect HTTP_PROXY, HTTPS_PROXY, and NO_PROXY environment variables.

☑ Add a custom proxy configuration

Proxy Type	☑ HTTP	☑ HTTPS
Proxy Server	127.0.0.1	: 8080 ⬍
Proxy Auth ❶	◯ OFF	
Username	Username	
Password	Password	🗡
Proxy Bypass	Enter comma separated hosts to bypass proxy settings. Example: 127.0.0.1, localhost, *.example.com	

Figure 10-3. *Configuring the proxy in the Postman tool*

Now that we are done with the configuration on the Postman side, we need to ensure that the right proxy configuration is also done on the Burp Suite Side. To ensure the correct proxy is configured in the Burp Suite, navigate to the Proxy tab and Options as shown in Figure 10-4, and ensure the IP address and port number match to what was configured earlier in Postman.

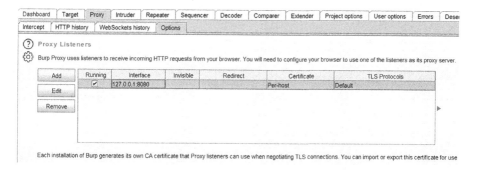

Figure 10-4. *Setting up the Burp Suite proxy listener*

Once both the Postman and Burp Suite are configured to work together, all the traffic generated from Postman will now pass through Burp Suite. This is very similar to how we configured our browsers to work along with Burp Suite.

Now that we have seen how to configure the Postman to work along with Burp Suite, we'll see how the reverse works; that is, how do we export data from Burp Suite into the Postman for selective testing?

While the Burp Suite Repeater and Intruder serve most of the purposes for performing security testing of an API, there could be a need to test a particular API in the Postman interface. In such a case, it is possible to export the API request from Burp Suite into the Postman tool.

For exporting an API request from Burp Suite to the Postman, we would need to install an extension called 'Postman Integration'. Simply navigate to the Extender tab and open the 'BApp Store' and install the 'Postman Integration' extension as shown in Figure 10-5.

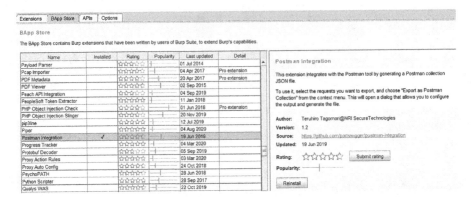

Figure 10-5. *Installing the Postman Integration extension in the Burp Suite through BApp Store*

Once the extension is installed:

1. Go to the Target tab,

2. Select the request you want to export to Postman,

3. Right-click on the request to be exported,

4. Select option 'Export as Postman Collection' as shown in Figure 10-6.

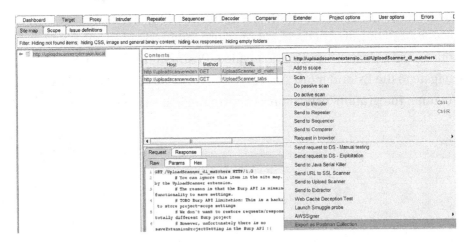

Figure 10-6. *Exporting requests in the Burp Suite as Postman collection*

A new window will pop up, as shown in Figure 10-7. Enter the required Collection Name and Folder name and click on the Export button. The collection would then be exported and saved to the specified location.

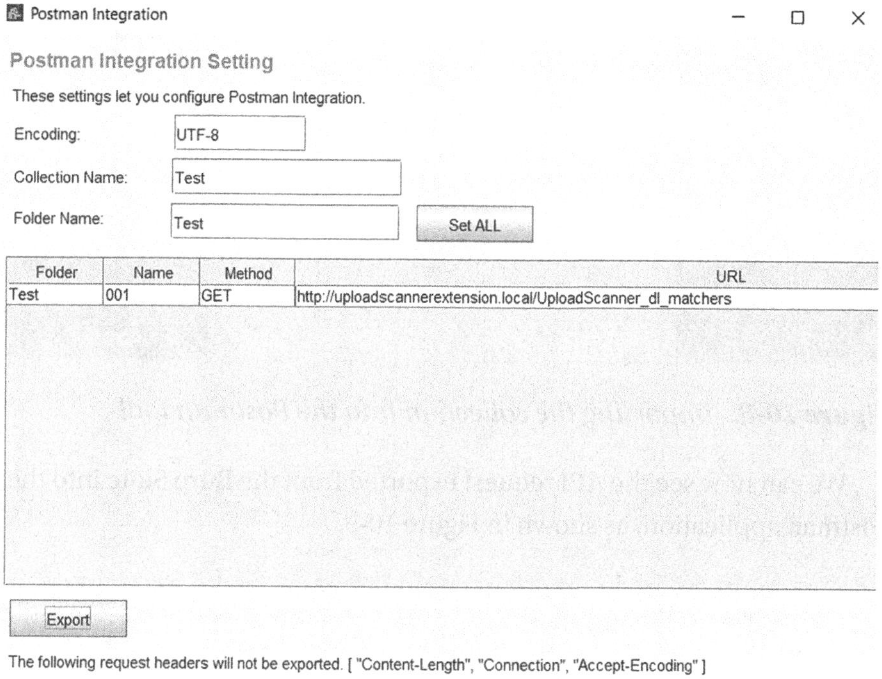

Figure 10-7. *Configuring the Postman integration settings*

Next, open the Postman application and click on Import, as shown in Figure 10-8. Click on choose files and select the file that we exported from Burp Suite earlier.

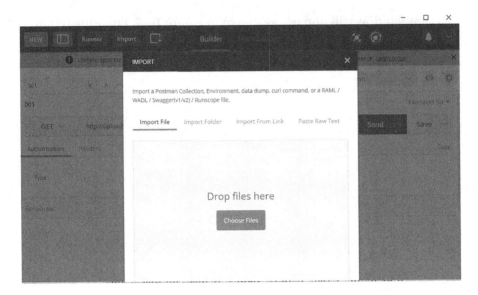

Figure 10-8. *Importing the collection into the Postman tool*

We can now see the API request exported from the Burp Suite into the Postman application, as shown in Figure 10-9.

Figure 10-9. *Collection imported in the Postman tool*

Mobile Application Security Testing with Burp Suite

In the previous section, we saw how Burp Suite could be configured along with the Postman to perform security testing on APIs. In this section, we'll have an overview of how we could leverage the Burp Suite capabilities for performing security testing of Mobile Applications.

Before we get into further details about Mobile Application security testing, it is important to understand the fact that the Burp Suite literally acts and serves as an HTTP proxy. This means we can effectively use Burp Suite for performing security testing on any device or application that interacts over HTTP or HTTPS protocol.

Mobile applications are no different; they use the same HTTP / HTTPS protocol for communication; hence that traffic can be routed through the Burp Suite just like any other regular web application. Figure 10-10 shows a mobile application client (the equivalent of the browser on PC), which is passing all the traffic through Burp Suite to the Application Server.

Figure 10-10. *Connecting mobile application to the Burp Suite*

We'll now see how we can configure Burp Suite to work along with the mobile application. First, we need to ensure that the correct Burp Suite proxy is set to listen on all interfaces. To do so, navigate to the Proxy ➤ Options tab, as shown in Figure 10-11.

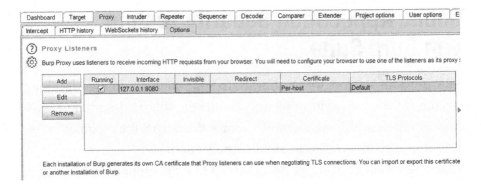

Figure 10-11. *Setting up the Burp Suite proxy listener*

Now click on the 'Add' button, and a new window will pop up as shown in Figure 10-12. Configure the port number and select 'Bind to address' as 'All interfaces' and click 'OK'.

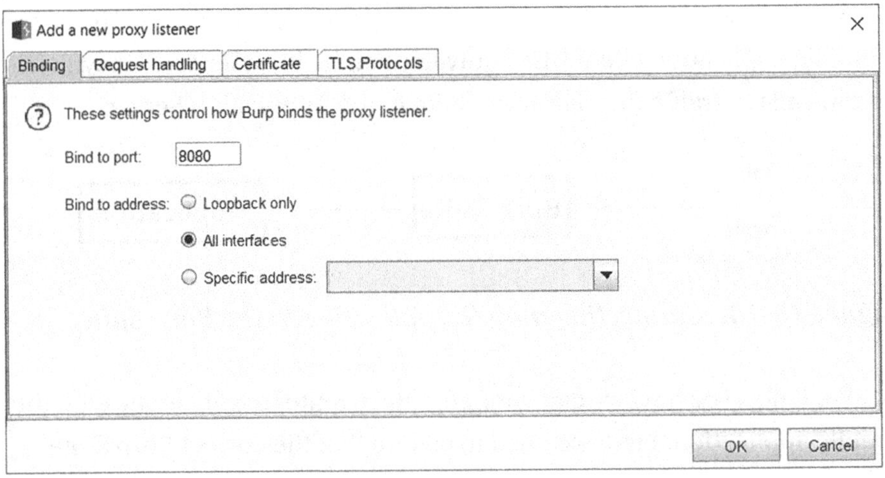

Figure 10-12. *Setting up the Burp Suite proxy listener*

Now notice the proxy listener section as shown in Figure 10-13, which lists the interface as '*:8080'.

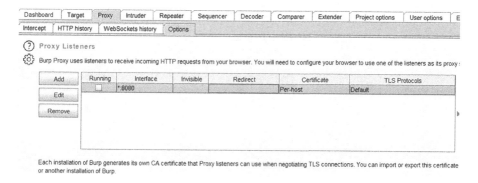

Figure 10-13. *Setting up the Burp Suite proxy listener*

Now that we have configured the Burp Suite proxy to listen on port 8080 on all available interfaces, we'll move ahead to the mobile device configuration.

It is important to note that in order to configure the mobile device to work along with Burp Suite, both the system running the Burp Suite and the mobile device need to be in the same logical network. The simplest way to achieve this is by connecting the mobile device and the system running Burp Suite to the same Wireless Access Point. Once the mobile device and the system running Burp Suite are connected to the same network, we need to configure the network settings on mobile to use Burp Suite as a proxy.

To configure the network proxy on the mobile device, go to the Wireless Settings and select the Wireless Network that you are connected to, as shown in Figure 10-14.

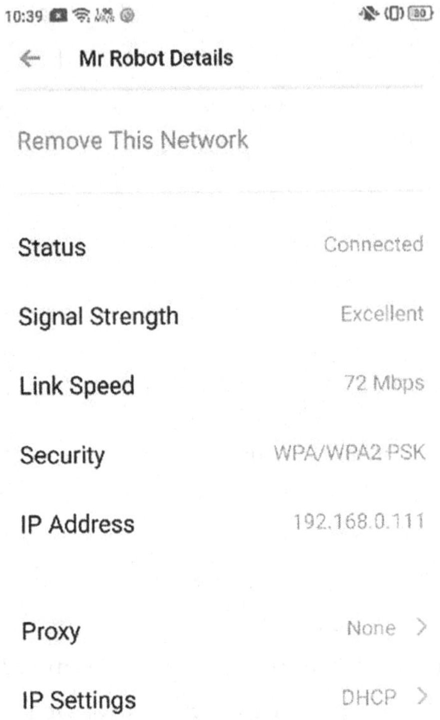

10:39 📷 📶 ⊛   🔕 ◁》📶

← | **Mr Robot Details**

Remove This Network

Status	Connected
Signal Strength	Excellent
Link Speed	72 Mbps
Security	WPA/WPA2 PSK
IP Address	192.168.0.111
Proxy	None >
IP Settings	DHCP >

Figure 10-14. *Configuring network proxy on mobile device*

Now click on the Proxy option, and a new configuration window will open as shown in Figure 10-15.

10:39 📷 📶 ⊛   🔕 ◁》📶

← | **Proxy**

None	⊙
Manual	○
Auto-Config	○

Figure 10-15. *Configuring network proxy on mobile device*

By default, the network proxy is set to 'None.' We need to change this to 'Manual,' as shown in Figure 10-16.

Figure 10-16. *Configuring network proxy on mobile device*

Now that we have changed the Proxy type to manual, we need to enter the IP address of the system where Burp Suite is running along with the port number on which the Burp Suite proxy service is listening to, as shown in Figure 10-17.

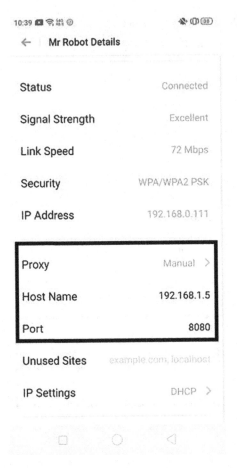

Figure 10-17. *Configuring network proxy on mobile device*

Once the manual proxy has been configured, all the traffic originating from the mobile application would now be routed through Burp Suite. Once the requests are in Burp Suite, they can be tampered with Repeater or Intruder just like any other regular HTTP request.

It's important to note two points with regard to performing security testing on mobile applications using Burp Suite:

1.   The Burp Suite can only help to execute manual
     security tests on the mobile application and, to
     a certain extent, perform dynamic application
     security testing.

2.   The exact process of configuring the network proxy
     on mobile devices varies as per the type and version
     of the operating system they run on. However, at a
     high level, the process would be similar to what we
     discussed in this section.

Security Testing Workflow with Burp Suite

Throughout the book, we have seen all aspects of Burp Suite and its
capabilities. We have seen various tools and utilities that are provided out
of the box as well as the use of third-party extensions, which significantly
enhance the Burp Suite capabilities.

Now, as we are at the end of the book, it would be worth summarizing
the workflow or approach for effectively using Burp Suite to test the
security of web applications.

Following is the phased approach that one can follow for effective use
of Burp Suite:

1.   **Get the right setup and configuration** – Before we
     actually begin using Burp Suite, it is important that
     it's set up and configured correctly.

     a. Make sure the right edition and the latest version of Burp
        Suite are being used.

     b. Configure the browser proxy settings to work along with Burp
        Suite.

     c. Install the Burp Suite CA certificate into the browser.

d. Configure the platform authentication, upstream proxy, and socks proxy as required.

e. Review and define the Burp Suite HotKeys.

f. Ensure automatic project backup is enabled and configured correctly.

g. Ensure project options like Timeouts, Hostname resolution, Out of Scope Requests, Redirections, TLS Configuration, Session Handling Rules, Cookie Jar, and Macros are configured as needed.

h. Make sure the proxy listener is configured and running properly.

i. Ensure all the required extensions are installed and loaded.

j. Check that the target application can be patched using the Burp Suite Infiltrator.

2. **Crawl and understand the application** – Once the Burp Suite is appropriately configured, it is important to crawl, surf, and browse the target application to know more about it.

a. Use the crawl function in the scanner to browse the application.

b. Make use of the content discovery feature.

c. Manually browse through the critical workflows.

d. Carefully observe the target tab and monitor the HTTP requests.

e. Find out and highlight interesting requests with parameters.

f. Use the analyze target feature to get an overview of the application scope.

g. Use engagement tools to find comments, scripts, and references.

h. Monitor the issues reported by the passive scans.

3. **Attack the application** – Now that we have done enough reconnaissance, it's time to attack selective application functionalities.

a. Run an audit task using the Burp Suite scanner.

b. Find out the interesting requests, especially the one with parameters, and send the request to the Repeater for further investigation.

c. Tamper and play around with the request, parameters, headers, and body using the repeater.

d. If a request and a parameter need to be tested against bulk payloads, then make use of Intruder.

e. Use the comparer to analyze and interpret differences in various responses.

f. Use a sequencer to test the strength of tokens.

g. Use the decoder for encoding or decoding any of the parameter values as required.

h. Test for the Clickjacking vulnerabilities using the Clickbandit tool.

i. Generate proof of concept for Cross-Site Request Forgery attack using the CSRF PoC generator.

j. Make use of the Burp Suite collaborator to effectively detect out-of-the band vulnerabilities like XML External Entity Injection (XXE) and Server Side Request Forgery (SSRF)

k. Monitor the issues pane under the target tab for all vulnerabilities found.

l. Select the required vulnerabilities and export them into an HTML report.

Summary

In this chapter, we saw how we could leverage Burp Suite capabilities for performing security testing on APIs as well as mobile applications. We also summarized the workflow that can be followed to make the best use of Burp Suite for web application security testing.

Exercises

1. Configure the Postman to work along with Burp Suite. Capture the API requests in Burp Suite and attack them using Repeater.

2. Test any of the target applications using the complete workflow discussed in this chapter.

Index

A

Active scanning, 112
API security testing, Burp Suite
    approaches, 148, 149
      Postman, 149, 150, 154
      Postman integration, 152–154
      proxy listener, 151
Application Programming
        Interfaces (APIs), 1, 147
Application security testing, 1, 4, 5
Application vulnerabilities, 2–4

B

Burp Suite, 5
    alternatives, 8, 9, 14
    browser, 15
    CA Certificate, 31, 32
    Chrome, 19
    Edge, 21
    editions, 6
    events, 16
    features, 7, 8
    Firefox, 17, 18
    hotkeys, 37, 38
    installation, 11

    need, 6
    Opera, 22
    options
      Cookie Jar monitors, 46, 47
      hostname resolutions, 42, 43
      macros, 47
      Out-of-scope request, 44, 45
      redirections, 45, 46
      timeouts, 42
    performance feedback, 41
    platform authentication, 33, 34
    project backups, 39
    proxy server, 35, 36
    Rest API, 39–41
    SOCKS proxy, 36, 37
    system proxy, 23, 24
    types of downloads, 12, 13
    useful features, 9, 10
    website, 16
Burp Suite extender
    APIs, 143
    BApp Store, 132–136
    extensions, 131
    manual installation, 136–139
    settings, 140–142
    useful extensions, 142, 143

© Sagar Rahalkar 2021
S. Rahalkar, *A Complete Guide to Burp Suite*,
https://doi.org/10.1007/978-1-4842-6402-7

Printed in the United States
By Bookmasters